I0759387

Make Do with What You Have

100 Delicious
New Recipes from
Favorite Old-School Meals

MAKE DO *with* What You Have

KARDEA BROWN

AMISTAD
An Imprint of HarperCollins*Publishers*

i dedicate

this book to my
loving husband, Bryon,
with whom I'm excited
to share a lifetime of
love, laughter, and
delicious meals.

contents

introduction

I'M NOT JUST FROM THE SOUTH, as in born and raised—I'm about as country as can be. And I'm proud of it. So imagine me, a twenty-something-year-old lil' country girl, leaving the simple Southern comfort of my childhood for the whirligig hustle-bustle—and cold—of the New York–New Jersey area. It wasn't because I didn't cherish my Geechee roots. Growing up near Wadmalaw Island, South Carolina, is not only the foundation of my professional cooking life as Delicious Miss Brown: It has shaped me culturally and spiritually. But like any young person, I reached a point where I felt like it was time for me to fly the nest and make my way in the world.

I don't regret my bold move. From my small New Jersey apartment, the bright lights of the big city were sure looking pretty. But I do recall plenty an evening when I had but a can of Libby's corn in the cupboard—that I was beyond grateful for, I might add. It just meant I'd need to get extra creative that night. Mind you, this was around 2013, when the average inflation rate was about 1.5 percent. (Now it's closer to 2.5 percent.) Still, the struggle was real. I didn't have the expertise or life experience to know that the US economy is cyclical. But what I did know served me well. I'm here to tell you, cousins: Trouble won't last always. I've lived that truth.

So I would gather up some coins, head to the store, and figure out what I could come up with. Because you know a country girl like me is gonna make a good meal. And guess what? I always ended up surprising myself. The thrill of my ingenuity was almost as filling as my dinner. For example, I might happen upon a "manager's special" that wasn't advertised in the circular, or maybe I'd find some slightly bruised produce that was marked down. That's when I'd skip home and dance into my cozy kitchen; cue up a get-right tune, like Mary J. Blige's "Just Fine" ("No time for mopin' around; are you kidding? . . . 'cause I'm winning"); and get cooking. Chop up some green pepper, throw in the neck bone I scored on sale, make a little pan gravy, put it all over a bed of rice. And *BAM*! (Only God's plan would have me quoting Emeril Lagasse years before even dreaming of a cooking career!) For around $10, I had myself a deliciously healthy and gorgeous meal, layered with flavor and brimming with vibrant color and fresh seasoning.

I was still in college when the iconic song "Empire State of Mind" came out. I can't say the song was a conscious influence, but on some level I think Alicia Keys's words hit like a clarion call to my restless young soul. And once I finished my undergraduate studies, I decided to set out for that "concrete jungle where dreams are made of." I was going to put my psychology degree to work and change the world—and you couldn't tell me otherwise. From childhood, I was that kid whose heart bled for the underdog. Maybe it had something to do with growing up in the church. More than likely my empathy was bred from traditional Gullah communal culture. With a tender soul paired with formal studies, I'd help save all the people, including myself.

Looking back, the bold move to relocate to the big city pretty much lived up to the hype in my head. City life scratched that itch for adventure and novelty. The culture. The diversity. The hustle. The excitement. I wasn't smack-dab in the center of things—after all, your baby girl had baby funds—but on the outskirts, which gave me a familiar sense of the provincial lifestyle I was accustomed to. I settled into an apartment about thirteen miles from Manhattan in Bayonne, New Jersey—a largely working-class city with a rich industrial history, especially in shipbuilding and manufacturing. Bayonne sits along the Hudson River and has a stunning waterfront view of the Manhattan skyline. Each day I traveled, on public transportation of course, about five or six miles to Saint Peter's University, where I was enrolled in a competitive master's degree program.

If you're anything like me, a hardcore music lover—sometimes lyrics hit with such force that you literally feel them in your bones. Alicia Keys told no lies. Trust and believe, cousins. Just trust and believe. Everything in and around New York truly feels kind of magical. And the go-getter energy starts to pulse through your body. Coming from the sleepy, cozy pace of the South, I found that all the hustle-bustle really set my soul on fire. I loved it!

But you know ya girl will always keep it real. I might tell you a joke, but I'll never tell you a lie. In spite of the big lights that inspire. and even though no other place could ever compare, on the flip side of the limelight and the city that never sleeps? Baybeee—life was HARD!

I mean after all, I wasn't a famous singer like Alicia Keys. Yes, I did come for school, but Lord knows I had not graduated to the high life. I was, you know, regular—a working-class girl from Charleston, South Carolina. A proud do-gooder, a social worker, determined to right the wrongs for vulnerable populations. Grad school, thc long-held dream of a kid raised on the ideals of educational excellence, was expensive. Rent and utilities for my teaspoon-size apartment in Bayonne swallowed a heaping helping of my monthly income. And as a twenty-something fun-seeker, I wanted to "get through this thing called life" (dearly beloved) with some measure of joy—my spirit intact.

That meant I had to adjust my dreams to my new reality—quick, fast, and in a hurry. The joy of my big-city adventure didn't fade, but my old-school upbringing emerged in stark relief. All of the lessons my mother and grandmother had poured into me over the years suddenly began to have meaning and very practical resonance. They weren't just words, they were mantras:

- If you wanna act grown, be grown.
- The Lord will make a way out of no way.
- He will never give you more than you can bear.
- Don't be penny-wise and pound-foolish.
- You got McDonald's money?

Instinctively, I knew how to buck up—and with a swiftness. You hear me? It was the very first time that I was flat-out on my own. And adulting was definitely testing my mettle. Mom was nearly a thousand miles away, as was my grandmother and the rest of my tribe. I did make fast friends. The people in my new life as a transplant were lovely, something I think a lot of folks get wrong about big-city life. But there were no aunties, no play sisters and such who'd known me since I was knee-high to a grasshopper. I had to pull up my big-girl panties and figure out how to make ends meet.

Fortunately, you can take the girl out of the Gullah Sea Islands. But you cannot—will not—take the Gullah Sea Islands out of the girl. I never lost sight of the simple Gullah Geechee values I was brought up with. Even with meager resources—at one especially rough point I went from my friend's sofa, to my other friend's sofa, to my other-other friend's sofa—I managed to not only survive but thrive in the shadow of Lady Liberty.

Some of my biggest opportunities were born out of those challenging years. My creativity was on fire. And I built strong and lasting relationships that would change the trajectory of my entire life.

Instead of whining and crying about what wasn't working for me at that time, I maximized all the good things that were coming my way. And you know what I came to realize? *I had it going on!* Even if no one could see it but me. I was very proud of the life I was building for myself, and it felt good to create my own idea of success. Some nights I might stop at a Redbox kiosk outside my local ShopRite grocery store to rent a movie. But, of course, splurges didn't happen regularly. My studies were just as enriching as I dreamed they would be. And although the salary was low, I soon had a job working with school-age kids at the kind of nonprofit community organization where I knew I could make a difference.

My resources were slim—in fact, in some ways, slimmer than ever. The job was stressful. So in addition to not having much money, I had very little time and energy. My working-girl era called for a new level of creativity when it came to my expenses. And I considered it a personal challenge to find new and inventive ways to pare down costs, including learning how to eat well and spend less. What can I say, some folks had Angry Birds or Tetris, but my game was figuring out how to make the most of all God blessed me with.

If you've been with me a while on this Food Network journey, then you know my story as well as my glory. You know that it was precisely those hard times that led to my career success at the Food Network. Back in the day, life as a TV chef had never even entered my mind. I wasn't thinking about cooking as anything more than a way to eat. I believe I was born with a servant's heart. And the only goal I had when I left South Carolina was furthering my education and helping as many folks as possible. As far as I was concerned, I'd already found career success. Children's social services unlocked a long-held passion, and I considered it a privilege to be working for Big Brothers Big Sisters. Here I was, only twenty-five years old, and in my mind I was *winning*! Yep, I had a small apartment. And yes, my job was very stressful some days. See, I soon learned that as much as I *wanted* to help people and as hard as I'd studied to address societal issues, there were some problems—no, make that *lots* of problems—lil' ole Kardea could not solve simply with her hard-earned degree and heart of service.

On those days, when the pressure of lifting people up got me down, I'd find solace in my kitchen. Not intentionally—I can't even say I knew that's what I was doing. It was instinctive, I suppose. Cousins, I really can't explain it. All I can tell you is that the way some people might retreat to a bubble bath or their favorite watering hole, I would find myself at the stove with some Jill Scott, Anita Baker, or whoever the mood called for playing in the background—just whipping and sautéing to my heart's content. And my boyfriend at the time—bless his heart—took note of my joy. He saw that cooking seemed to set my soul on fire. And what's so funny is that I really didn't think there was anything remarkable happening at all. I mean, working through recipes and playing with flavors was a simple pleasure. Sure, it felt good to create delicious meals and have this special person in my life eat the food and praise my skills. But I didn't see what he saw: a person truly in her happy place, a zone where I spent time alone in a get-right—almost spiritual—headspace. And totally unbeknownst to me, he captured me on film stirring up a pot of I-don't-even-know-what and sent the video to the Food Network for a guest spot on a new show. Out of the hundreds, if not thousands, of videos submitted, guess whose tape the producers chose? Can you even believe it? No broadcast experience. No professional chef experience. No restaurant experience. No on-air-of-any-kind experience. How could something so random change my entire life?

If you grew up in the church the way I did, I know you've sat through many a sermon where the pastor takes his *time* to break down the principles of God's will and His grace. And here I was living it. I'm not going to start preaching up in here, at least not right this minute. But cousins, I get goose bumps when I think about how the Lord had been all the while ordering my steps. Because, as many of us know, we don't serve a random God, right? All of those years, He was preparing me. And I didn't have a clue.

I was raised to believe His word. God's timing is not our timing. His ways are not our ways. What seemed from the outside like a "suddenly . . ."

plot twist in a book had been part of the story all along. And baby, once I had my Ephesians "foretaste" moment, ya girl never looked back. But don't get it twisted. I'm not saying the rest came easy. It took four and a half years from that first surprise call from the Food Network to get to *Delicious Miss Brown.*

And I am a living witness to the power of destiny. Whether you have a burning dream inside your soul or if you're not yet quite sure of your purpose in life, trust the process and follow your heart. Because God is the master author of "suddenly." Trust me when I tell you that there is something unique in all of us—and it's waiting to be tapped.

Your something may not be my something. But what I absolutely know for sure is that no talent, no experience, no passion we have inside of us is wasted—no matter how long it may take to be revealed to the outside world. Don't give up, cousins!

Some people are born knowing their purpose. And they spend their entire lives building toward it brick by brick. Most of us don't have it like that. We simply keep putting one foot in front of the other—doing what we feel is the right thing or pursuing a piece of our purpose in the way that we know best. Although I knew I wanted to help people to change folks in some way, it took God's redirection for me to begin to see how He meant for me to accomplish that.

Cousins, I surely don't know what the future holds, but I know who holds the future. This positivity doesn't come from a know-it-all place or self-help guru kinds of formulas—I highly doubt there are any ten steps, or whatever, that lead to the life of your dreams. Nope. I just have faith. I know firsthand—in fact, I am a living witness—that your purpose will be revealed. And I hope that, whether you enjoy cooking or you just like eating, my story somehow feeds you. I promise you, I am no more extraordinary than you are.

Sometimes, especially the way our culture is set up to worship material things as social media drowns us in images of "success" and baller lifestyles, we can forget what's really real. And we forget that things take time.

Now ask yourself—and this is the really important part—what are you doing while you wait? I certainly do love God. He is faithful. But if there's one thing you need to understand, it's that He *will* make you wait. God's timing is, well—it's different from ours. Some of the practices I established over the years, I think, helped prepare me. You can try them too. Before I share them, though, I want to make something very clear: There are many God-fearing people who say, while you wait you should "just pray without ceasing." And while I believe 1,000 percent in the power of prayer, I also know that period can be a difficult time. And it's not always easy to be patient.

I can be an anxious girlie myself, and I'm pretty sure I'm not the only one. So I want you to know I see you. No matter where you are in your faith walk—and maybe you don't even have a faith walk, or even a faith crawl—waiting is not idling; there's a lot we can all do in that meantime and in-between time. Here's my take: Work hard to get your life right, your mind right, and your spirit right. We all know that saying: "If you stay ready, you won't need to get ready." There's a *lot* of truth in that.

Let me tell you, on my own journey, once I got a nibble of cooking on a show and saw what a life as a TV chef might look like, no one could tell me I wasn't ready right then and there. That's how badly I wanted it. But things didn't go down like that. And in hindsight, I'm very grateful. I needed to learn so much about the business side of television and the technical aspects of cooking. And if I hadn't been forced to learn those things, I don't think I'd have found success. I definitely wouldn't have been as confident in my ability to carry a show.

So whether you want to level up at work and land a big promotion, or succeed in your business or personal life, use that period of time that you're waiting to get prepared. Be superproductive so you're ready for your blessings. Of course, everything is not for everybody. Just remember there is nothing too small, too corny, or too "out there" if it helps you stay the course, de-stress, and keep the faith. And honestly, I could talk *all* day about some of the things in my toolbox that have helped me, and continue to help me, stay even-keeled. Some are really simple.

- **Vision board.** I am a firm believer in visualization. And I put together some pretty elaborate vision boards to set my intentions and literally see where I want to go. There are books and kits you can get at craft stores like Michaels. Or you can go digital with tools like Canva. They have a template for every kind of board you can think of.
- **Write it down.** Pro tip: You don't need to be Toni Morrison to sit down and journal. Just put something down on paper. Maybe you don't have the business plan just yet. The details might be sketchy right now. It's okay. I journaled my goals, ideas, and passions every day, even though I didn't have a concrete plan.
- **Be still.** I realize you may be giving me the screw face right now. And yes, I know you see me out here ripping and running half the time. But I do find time to decompress. It's important, as old Southern folks say, to "go somewhere and sit down" for lots of reasons. We need to shut out the noise of social media, friends, work, family—and step back to try to get a high-level view of the big picture. Otherwise, the small stuff will bury you.
- **Look back at it.** Okay, now before you go *there*, let me explain: This is about reflection. Take some time occasionally to appreciate how far you've come. Seriously, I get that we all want the dream to happen yesterday. But that's not realistic. If we're going to stay fired up, we have to celebrate ourselves along the way. Say it out loud: "I may not be where I want to be, but thank God I am not where I was."
- **Let the music play.** Our jams have power, and from the time I was a little girl in church feeling the spirit move during worship,

I've known the power of song. Get into it, if you haven't already, to lift your spirits and shift your heart. I mix gospel, R & B, hip-hop—whatever I need to speak to me. If you're feeling discouraged, there are few better remedies than Norman Hutchins's "God's Got a Blessing (with My Name on It!)" or the Clark Sisters, in my opinion.

- **Use your words.** Cousins, we must speak life over our hopes. Affirm yourself, please. Personally, I lean into the word of God. This is one of my favorites: "Weeping may endure for a night, but joy comes in the morning." If you don't know scripture, you can swap any positive affirmations that suit you: "I got this" or "I am enough."
- **Show up.** This is your life, cousins. You owe it to yourself to be as present as possible. We *all* have those days when we want to hide under the covers. And I'm not going to lie—every once in a while, if that's the break you need, then you need to take it because rest is a big part of what it takes to show up as your best, authentic self. I believe rest can also help us remember who we are. That way you can get up, dust yourself off, and step out into your boldness.

We each have something that is uniquely ours to share with the world. Some of us need a little while to discover that something. And that was me. I knew I was proud of my Geechee heritage—and our food being the cornerstone of that culture—but as a young person I didn't fully appreciate just how special and rich our traditions were. Believe it or not, it wasn't until college that I learned that not everyone cooked fresh food on the regular. My dorm mates were nuking everything you could think of, and I was amazed when I first got to campus. Seriously, I thought it was the wildest thing.

My storied heritage was so ingrained in me, it was like the air I breathed. Second nature. I knew it was a good thing, but I didn't know it was special-special—if that makes sense. Us Gullah Geechee folks are the descendants of those enslaved people who were brought to America from western and southwestern Africa, including Sierra Leone, Senegal, and Angola. We were amazing farmers—lima beans, okra, and tomatoes—who worked the coastal plantations along South Carolina and Georgia. Gullah Geechee people lived off the land, incorporating oysters, turtles, and shrimp into our cuisine. And man, did we know how to cultivate some rice. That's important, because it takes great skill.

On some level, I guess I assumed the world knew all about how Gullah folks preserved so much of our Africanness. How we were stolen by enslavers and brought to the shores of the Atlantic—largely from rice-growing regions of West Africa. How, even in the present day, Geechees are steeped in many of the cultural rituals of West Africa that our enslaved descendants had held on to for centuries. Our language, for example, a creole patois, deliberately confused the white plantation rulers and any outsiders—and also created a way to communicate among tribes who spoke different languages. After all, they had to come up with one common language. Spirituality also ran deep—mostly Christian beliefs but with elements of some African practices—and incorporated values like community over individuality, respect for elders, kinship bonds, and honoring the extension of life as well as the afterlife. And, of course, the foodways are the centerpiece of Gullah culture.

It's no secret that what Americans, and people around the world really, think of today as Southern soul food came out of the ingenuity of our enslaved ancestors, who took the sad scraps, damaged crops, and whatever else they could get and transformed them into delicious meals. Well, for my people—Geechee folks—it goes even deeper. Because we were surrounded by the ocean, the meals included lots of fresh seafood as well as vegetables, fruits, and rice—oh, so much rice. Then, on top of all that goodness, we had the foods imported from Africa during the slave trade. I'm talking okra, yams, peas, hot peppers, sesame "benne" seeds, sorghum, and watermelon. Let's not forget that the land along the Atlantic was also populated with Indigenous people. And they were living off the land way before we got there. Those Native Americans introduced goodies like corn, squash, tomatoes, and all kinds of delicious berries.

With a food history so layered and beautiful, I could never have imagined living off of microwavable meals. I'd grown up in the kitchen—the sometimes-pesky sous-chef to my mom and grandmother. I watched them make Gullah classics like red rice, okra stew, and sweet potato pone with superfresh superingredients, sometimes plucked from the garden that very day. If you didn't have a garden, you patronized local farmers who brought fresh foods to open-air markets or drove trucks full of goodness through the neighborhood. (The watermelon man was always in demand.) Cousins, my Geechee folks—from enslavement times to the present day—never needed a trendy label like "farm-to-table." We aren't new to this; we're true to this! Wholesome food is the cornerstone of Gullah culture.

So when my mom worked late or, like most parents, had to shuttle me from cheerleading practice to soccer practice, she never dreamed of leaning on fast-food chains. Not to say that we *never* hit up Mickey D's, but it was rare. For her busiest days, Mom had a bunch of grab-and-go meals she'd make: sausage-egg-and-cheese sandwiches or cucumber spaghetti salad. I'm certainly not judging anyone who relies on prepackaged food, but the reality is, those kinds of convenience meals come at a high cost. And my mother had to stretch her dollars to give me the life she wanted me to have.

Growing up, I knew on a very rudimentary level that we were working-class folks of very average means. Clearly, we weren't wealthy, but we were also far from poor. What I know now that my younger self could never have understood is the Great Recession, which like any seismic shift in the global economy rippled across many industries. When I was coming up, I know the pain was felt by people we knew in manufacturing and construction. And the recovery was slow, slow, slow.

Sometimes my mom worked two jobs—especially during the holiday season, when she'd usually take on a seasonal retail position, like at Stein Mart or Value City, to put some of my wishlist items under the Christmas tree. Mom was usually pretty clear about what we could and couldn't afford. But every year she surprised me with some of the holiday delight she made happen.

I truly never thought, "Oh, pity me," or looked at our occasional bank account limitations as a burden. From a very young age, my Spidey Senses could tell sometimes that my mom's pocketbook was lighter than she let on. During some back-to-school seasons, we went shopping and brought all the shiny new purchases home with us. Other times, school clothes were put on layaway. Maybe instead of paying the phone bill in full, she'd arrange a payment plan. Whatever and however Mom had to cut corners, she did so—and with a grace and a spirit of gratitude that I suppose I internalized as the natural order of things.

And no matter how much or how little we had during certain seasons, we felt blessed to help others. Our next-door neighbor was a single dad, and whatever we had—we shared. In fact, if anybody anywhere in our community was going through a rough patch, Ma sent me to their house to offer a plate brimming with home-cooked food. I remember that my mom, and everyone else I knew, almost always cooked a lot of food at once—enough to last a couple of meals, not just one. Even my grandmother, who lived alone, cooked big pots of okra stew or lima beans and neck bones.

When I got older, I realized that those summers spent with my grandmother served two purposes. Yes, those ten weeks or so gave me and Grandma time to bond, but they also gave Ma a bit of a break. There were times when maybe she'd be furloughed or get fewer hours if retailing slowed down, but Mom always worked—and worked hard.

Still, we had a great life. Just because my mom couldn't afford to buy me a closet full of name-brand clothes, it doesn't mean I went to school looking shabby. Cousins, my 'fits were *cute*! And just because she wasn't buying filet mignon each week, doesn't mean we didn't enjoy good meals with delicious cuts of beef seasoned to perfection.

So as a grown-up, I never freaked out over making ends meet. My own experience has taught me that being broke doesn't mean being broken. And delayed doesn't mean denied. There was nothing scary to me about squeezing a dollar till George Washington was crying! In fact, there were many times when I could hear my mother's words ringing in my head. Has that ever happened to you? Those well-worn quips and sayings that made me want to roll my eyes as a child begin to make more and more sense:

- He supplies our every need.
- You're stronger than you know.
- Make do with what you have.

I know I am not the only one. Although I'm a Food Network star now and I've been materially blessed over the course of the past few years, in my spirit I am—and will always be—cautious and thoughtful about the way I approach spending. In my life, whether it's my money, my time, or my energy, I don't take things for granted. Maybe it's where I came from. My mom was busy. The people I grew up with were much like her—hardworking. I know that God's got me, but I also know that it's my responsibility to be a good steward.

Do you know the biblical Parable of the Talents? It's always stuck with me. I promise, even if you're not a Christian, it will make sense. The story, as I learned it, is basically saying: We are privileged to have God-given talents or resources, gifts, and even opportunities to work in service of Him. In the Bible, "talents" can be interpreted as money, but it can also mean "sense." I won't go into the entire parable here. What I learned in Bible study, though, and remember to this day is that three men were given talents, according to their ability: one got five talents, one got two talents, and the last one got only one. Each man chose to use their talents as they saw fit. And to the Lord's disappointment, only two made good faithful choices—getting a 100 percent profit on their talents. One held on to his little talent and buried it somewhere for safekeeping and gained no return on the Lord's investment. He was scolded and punished.

That will never be me, cousins. The Parable of the Talents shows us that to whom much is given, much is expected. I'm forever deeply grateful. And I know that no matter how far you—my loving cousins—may ride with me and support the successful TV enterprise of *Delicious Miss Brown*, Kardea Brown will forever be *that* girl. The one who knows how to make a dollar out of fifteen cents. The one who knows the best things in life are not things at all. And importantly, the one who is all the way real. I get it. I get *you*. And I got you.

It's an honor and a stone-cold blast—c'mon *Soul Train* lovers—for me to be able to share the joys of good food and family cooking. Being in your homes through the Food Network and meeting you—whether on IG or IRL—has blessed me in countless ways. One thing you probably know about me by now is that joy and practicality are the main ingredients in any truly soul-filled recipe. Everything starts there. I'll never stand in my kitchen and yammer on and on about an amazing meal that requires fifty-eleven high-end products or expensive, hard-to-find spices.

But like you, recently I started to notice that even simple dishes were getting more and more challenging to prepare. The cost of chicken was climbing. And one of the most basic staples in any home—eggs, if you could find any on store shelves, were sky-high.

Cousins, we aren't imagining this thing. It's not just chicken or just eggs: Prices across the board have been steadily creeping up. That supermarket sticker shock is real. Food prices across the country soared by nearly 24 percent from 2020 to 2024, according to the US Department of Agriculture.*

Don't think I don't know that inflation has families across America in a choke hold. I mean, it is hard out here in these streets—and by streets, I mean the grocery aisles. I see you up in Piggly Wiggly, Ralphs, and Publix. And I see the prices jumping like june bugs on porch lights from one

* Victoria Davidenko and Megan Sweitzer, "Food Prices and Spending," US Department of Agriculture, Economic Research Service, February 14, 2025, https://www.ers.usda.gov/data-products/ag-and-food-statistics-charting-the-essentials/food-prices-and-spending.

week to the next. None of us can afford to take these kinds of blows to our pocketbooks. And we shouldn't have to.

It's frustrating when Bryon says he's got a taste for a rib-eye steak and I go to the meat department only to find out the cut I need is four dollars higher than it was just a few weeks ago. You all know I love my hubby, but he and I are kindred souls in more ways than one. We both have common sense. That's when I get creative and think, *How can I fix something close to the flavors he craves for less money?*

Food, for me, is and always will be about family. What we're all experiencing right now in this difficult economy is not new. I've shared the many ways my mom and my grandma worked to make ends meet. They shopped carefully at the grocery store, then came home and worked wonders in the kitchen to make delicious family meals.

Well, the way I see it, you're my family too. And it just doesn't sit right in my spirit to not help you do the same. Think of me as your culinary spirit animal. I know you love food like I do, but it's not realistic, or sustainable, for any of us to be out here alone racking our brains and stretching our pockets. During the COVID pandemic and in the difficult times that followed, I think we've all struggled—some more than others. I won't pretend to be an economist. But I know firsthand that shortages, supply-chain problems, and corporate greed—yes, I said it—are doing a number on our finances.

Now, sadly, I don't have any tricks to help you make rent. But I can come through in the food department. There are tricks I can share that will help you save money on your grocery bill. Importantly, there are also shortcuts you can take before you even get to the checkout line. For example, I know this may seem tedious and old-school, but we're going to bring back shopping lists. You can scribble on the back of your utility bill or keep a running list of items in your notes app. And speaking of apps, don't sleep on downloading local grocery store apps. You'll get extra savings as well as rewards points. And many include a list section as well as reminders that tell you when you may be running out of your favorite items.

With these kinds of moves, you'll be saving time, money, and aggravation. I'm convinced that some of the biggest barriers to cooking at home can be addressed with practical steps that demystify the whole process. Don't laugh, cousins—I didn't make up the name—but there was a 2024 study called "Clueless Cook"** that backs up everything my followers on social media have said over the years:

- More than half of Americans (54 percent) say they are not proficient in the kitchen.
- 54 percent cite lack of time as their biggest barrier to becoming a better cook.
- 49 percent cite a lack of motivation (laziness).
- 34 percent say they have limited kitchen resources.

Despite the fact that they're not cooking for themselves, we know, of course, that these folks are eating. For me, here's where the study gets really good: The study also found that

- Nearly half (48 percent) follow food influencers on social media.
- Roughly three-quarters watch cooking videos.
- And 73 percent say their parents were good cooks.

I know many of you *want* to cook more often. It can be daunting when it seems that doing so feels out of reach. If you recognize yourself in these statistics, we're about to change the game! We're going to get through this together. And cousins, I guarantee you will feel full and satisfied once you learn to make do with what you have. I'm talking about the budget you have, the skills you have, and the ingredients you have—all the resources need to be taken into account.

Let's do this—together.

** "Clueless Cooks: The 2024 report," The Linz Shop, accessed March 7, 2025, https://shop.linzheritageangus.com/clueless-cooks-report.

ONE
getting started

WHEN I TRAVEL AROUND VARIOUS CITIES, I hear a lot from people who grew up as I did. Maybe not exactly the way I did, steeped in Gullah culture. But y'all tell me that watching *Delicious Miss Brown* is like a letter from home—as us country folks like to say. That's a high compliment, of course, because it's my deepest mission to touch that part of viewers that recalls comfort and family and the simple pleasures of good food.

What I also get a lot is people who say, "I really want to cook, Kardea, but I can't because . . ." Different reasons follow that statement, but they can be boiled down into one simple fact: They can't figure out a way to do it consistently. They may tell me some version of one or two things: "Oh, I can never think of what to cook—looking at your recipes I get overwhelmed" or "I would cook more often, but with work and family obligations I don't have time to shop for fresh groceries." Let me put you on.

Usually, when we say we don't know what to cook, it's shorthand for "I don't have the things on hand I would need to put a meal together." Naturally, that leads to feeling discouraged and unmotivated. It makes perfect sense. So don't be so hard on yourself. The same is true for people who think they don't have time to shop.

Cousins, there is no shame to my game. I bring you simple, home cooking by design. The last thing I want is for you to be tied to your stove all day long. The goal is to show you tasty food that anyone can prepare. I deliberately make sure that my recipes don't call for a lot of hard-to-find ingredients and that prep time is kept to a minimum. Then, after I show you step-by-step how to create the foods, the big reveal happens: My family and friends come out, and we get down, eating every morsel.

Now, I'm going to take you behind the scenes. Yes, my recipes are straightforward, but there are levels to everything. With some strategy and planning, you can succeed. Trust me on this: You have what it takes, cousins—you simply don't have all that you need to make good cooking happen. If you were a painter, you'd never think you could create a masterpiece without a range of brushes and the primary tools you'd need to practice your craft. The same is true with cooking. I am willing to bet, a dollar to a donut, that the missing key lies in what is—and what isn't—already in your cupboard.

We're about to get into it. Please understand that I'm not suggesting you go out and buy everything off your local grocer's shelves or splurge on fancy new pots and pans. But there are certain food items and cooking tools you will want to keep on hand and in good repair. You probably have some personal favorites—I know I do—and that's great. If you're able to round out what you already own with what I like to call a cook's starter set, it will truly pay for itself in a short period.

Cookware

There's no need to spend hundreds of dollars, but do get the best cookware you can afford. Heat distribution is a big deal—you want your food to cook evenly—and the quality of the materials does make a difference. You'll want the following:

- A heavy-duty skillet, preferably cast-iron, will conduct heat, sear, and fry foods better than a lightweight aluminum pan.
- A Dutch oven, which is capable of everything from slow cooking, braising, even frying.
- A stock pot, a versatile piece of cookware that every cook should have. Great for making large batches of soups, stews, and crab boils.

- A saucepan, in my humble opinion, a vital piece of cookware in the kitchen. It's used for a wide variety of cooking—including making sauces, soups, and stews—and simmering.

I'm not a big believer in kitchen gadgets. They can be nice to have, but I didn't grow up with peelers, presses, graters, and the like. I watched the women in my family wield a solid paring knife like a magic wand. You'll see me use a few gadgets when I'm cooking on the Food Network, but that's primarily because I want viewers to enjoy the food prep process as much as possible. You should invest in gadgets and cooking helpers at your own discretion. I will say it's great to see many manufacturers selling entire lines devoted to people of various abilities. The adaptive tools on the market now, like rocking knives and ergonomic spatulas, are awesome, especially for the elderly. They help make common, everyday kitchen activities—chopping, measuring, pouring, serving—easier for people who might have less strength or limited mobility from arthritis or any kind of disability.

Pantry Foods

How you slice and dice is up to you, of course. Whatever you plan to cook will require you to have certain staple foods on hand. Think of them as your accessories. Most of us get dressed every day and wear pretty similar clothes. Some days I may choose jeans and a sweater—with a pair of sneakers. You might wear jeans and a sweater with a pair of heels. And we'll both likely add personal touches like a pair of earrings, a certain jacket, or a handbag.

The cupboard is where you pull from to bring your own flavor to a meal. There are fundamental ingredients—like a pair of jeans—that everyone needs, but the way you play with them can depend on your personality. What I especially like is that these staples are relatively inexpensive and super accessible. I like to think of them as my ride-or-die items, because they're dependable and I use them so frequently.

Stock up on them so you never run out. Spices, obviously, will give you the versatility you need to zhuzh up an inexpensive cut of meat or transform a regular chicken cutlet from ordinary to ethnic fusion. Flour and cornstarch will thicken your gravies and sauces. And oils and vinegars can make the difference between a boring side salad and greens dressed deliciously for a healthy meal.

The items listed here are some of my personal favorites, but there are no hard-and-fast rules. You probably have a lot of these in your cupboard already, but do check expiration dates. It may take a while, but olive oil, breadcrumbs, and other pantry goods do go bad. If your cupboards are missing a few things, don't feel compelled to go out and buy everything at once. You can build up your supply of "basics" over time by buying one or two each week or so. Here's what you need to get good meals started. It's a good idea to always check and make note of what you need to restock before you do your regular grocery shopping.

Dry goods. Pound for pound, basics like oats and pasta are the most budget-friendly pantry items you can buy. And they go a long way. If you have room to store extra, you'll get great value from buying them in bulk, then putting them in airtight canisters or zip-top bags.

Baking powder
Baking soda
Cornstarch
Dry beans: black, white (cannellini, navy), kidney, garbanzo, lentils
Flour: all-purpose, self-rising
Pasta: macaroni elbow, spaghetti

Rice: long-grain white, parboiled, brown, wild, or jasmine
Rolled oats
Sugar: white, light and dark brown, confectioners' (powdered)
Yellow cornmeal

Vinegars and oils are an absolute must. Without them there is no dressing or sauces—no life to our dishes. Like James Brown, cousins, vinegars and oils are probably the hardest working ingredients in any kitchen, adding instant zest to your foods. Depending on our tastebuds, health choices, and other factors, we all have our go-to options. There is rarely a need to spend extra on fancy varieties, and most have a long shelf life. So stick to what you can afford, and I promise you can't go wrong.

Honey
Hot sauce
Mayonnaise*
Mustard: yellow, Dijon*
Oils: vegetable or canola, extra-virgin olive oil, nonstick cooking spray
Peanut butter*
Soy sauce*
Vinegar: apple cider, red wine, rice, balsamic
Worcestershire sauce*

*Refrigerate after opening

Herbs and spices are the workhorses in any kitchen—you already know! How you spice your food is extremely personal, so I can only give you a list of some of my go-to flavors. Spices have a fairly long shelf life and don't have an exact expiration date. If you suspect yours are past their prime, a sniff test will tell you if the oomph is still there. Cousins, if the smell is gone, so is the thrill—you probably won't fully taste that flavor in your food.

- Cayenne pepper
- Chili powder
- Cinnamon
- Cocoa powder
- Crushed red pepper
- Cumin
- Curry powder
- Garlic powder
- Italian seasoning
- Onion powder
- Salt (kosher salt)
- Smoked paprika
- Turmeric
- Vanilla extract
- Whole peppercorns

Tips for Saving Money

Now that we've reviewed what to buy, let's talk about *how* to buy. We can't control how high grocery prices will climb or how long inflation will last. What we can do—as best we can—is adapt to our new reality by setting up some habits that may help us save as much of our hard-earned money as possible. You may already be doing some, or even all, of these cost-saving techniques.

Think about upcoming meals. Hear me out: Planning out what you want to cook five to ten days ahead of time is a fail-safe way to watch your coins and make sure you've got everything you need to make the foods you know you and your family will enjoy. It's something I was raised to do, so it's second nature for me now as an adult. I will say, though, that for a lot of people I talk to nowadays, it's a bridge too far—folks feel like they don't have the time or headspace for this task. But my grandma always told me that if you want to get a different result, you will need to change what you do. At the very least, I suggest you land on a few meals you plan to cook over the course of the upcoming week.

Make a list and stick to it. Don't guess. Don't eyeball your fridge. Take account of both what you need for the meals you plan to cook and your general restocking needs. Without a list, a store filled with goodies—especially if you go in hungry, tired, or in a rush—can put a serious dent in your wallet. You will throw things you don't need into the cart—simply reacting to everything you see. For example, if yogurt is on sale for 50 percent off, it's not a good buy if you don't need it. And picking up lots of markdowns is going to sting when you get to checkout and discover you're way over budget.

Pro tip: Shop the perimeter of the grocery store for fresh produce, meats and fish, and dairy products. Try to avoid prepackaged items unless they are absolute must-haves. Precut veggies or shredded cheese can save you cooking time, but you're paying a higher price for that convenience. Opt for whole items, like fresh or frozen veggies and block cheese, to save money.

Shop around. Back in the day, I'd ride shotgun with my mom as she did the weekly grocery shopping. And this may be just me, but I loved every second of this admittedly mundane activity. The weekly sale circulars were held tighter than the Lost Ark of the Covenant as we went to various stores, depending on what was on sale and where. Cousins, this is no time to play favorites. I don't want you to burn a hole through your gas budget, but go where the sales are. And if you have an affinity for high-end grocery stores, you may want to consider switching to Aldi or Trader Joe's for certain products.

Join the loyalty program. I know, I know. It's no fun being hit with an onslaught of emails and text alerts from businesses we frequent. Understandably, many of us try to limit them. But do join grocery store loyalty programs; the benefits can outweigh the annoyance, and you can opt out of promotional materials. They are almost always free to join. And by signing up, you can get members-only discounts automatically at checkout—without clipping dozens of store coupons.

Clip coupons. Yes, it's totally old-school. But manufacturer coupons, found online or in newspapers and magazines, will help you save more money on top of the discounts offered at your local grocery store. So once you sign up for a grocery store's loyalty program, maximize your savings by clipping coupons for additional discounts. Source through the pages for deals that matter to you. Cut out any coupons, and save them for your next grocery run. Digital coupons are a great option too. Download your favorite grocery store's mobile app, browse the available discounts, and click to load coupons onto your digital loyalty card. Then, when you check out in store, the discounts will automatically be applied.

Join a wholesale club. They aren't cheap—the least expensive Costco membership, for example, is around sixty dollars annually—but depending on your family size and buying habits, bulk purchases can rack up big savings in the long run. With the upfront fee, this may not be an option for you, depending on your cash flow. And wholesale club shopping requires a degree of discipline. Even with lower-priced bulk buying, be sure to watch for sales and resist the urge to grab items on impulse.

Buy generic brands. Retailers are clever, and top brands pay for visibility. When you stroll the aisles of your favorite supermarket, remember that they are trying to tempt you to buy pricier name-brand items by placing them at eye level. Most of us aren't trying to linger in the market, so we take the bait and end up spending more money on high-cost items. But hold up. Train yourself to take just a minute to look at the top and bottom shelves. That's where you'll usually find generic brands, like the store's own brand. These products are going to be cheaper, and nine times out of ten, they'll taste just as good. Save yourself some cash next time you go shopping, and try a generic brand.

Miss Brown's House Seasoning "Big Batch"

This recipe makes a great big batch of my very own seasoning mix, which tastes good on practically everything! You'll see it used throughout this cookbook and in most of my recipes. It will last up to a year if stored in an airtight container.

Makes 1⅔ cups

- ⅓ cup garlic powder
- ⅓ cup onion powder
- ⅓ cup sweet paprika
- ⅓ cup kosher salt
- ⅓ cup freshly ground black pepper

In a small bowl, combine the garlic powder, onion powder, paprika, salt, and pepper. Store in an airtight container.

TWO

tasty cuts

IF YOU'RE A BEEF LOVER, I don't have to tell you how hard it's been to catch a break on price these days. I noticed the cost per pound rising dramatically several years ago due to drought and high grain costs. The US Bureau of Labor Statistics has tracked prices for sirloin steak and ground beef since the 1980s, and its data shows that prices were fairly consistent until the first summer of the COVID-19 pandemic.

But I'm here to tell you, cousins, that you don't need to break the bank on tenderloins and rib-eye steaks to get tasty beef meals. Sirloin tips, chuck roast, and even stew meat and ground beef can be very delicious options when done right. In this section, you'll find easy and fun ways to use all kinds of cuts. You know those cuts of meat that sit in the back of your freezer because you don't know what to do with them? We're putting an end to that right here and right now.

You can't tell me that my Lowcountry Low 'n' Slow Roast (page 39) with those onions, tomatoes, and carrots dancing together in the oven for three hours isn't the epitome of tenderness. Your family will love it. When you're not able to let a meal like that take its time—the Lowcountry Low 'n' Slow Roast is perfect for Sundays—check out my take on Grandma's Meatballs (page 42). You can get them on the table in just under thirty minutes. And adding a bit of ground pork really tops off the flavor.

Don't sleep on pork, my friends. Many of us don't eat a lot of it. But few dishes scream love and goodness like my Grilled "Poke" Chops (page 41).

Ground Beef Stir-Fry

Serves 3

½ cup water

½ cup low-sodium soy sauce

3 tablespoons packed light brown sugar

1 tablespoon cornstarch

4 cloves garlic, minced, or ½ to 1 teaspoon garlic powder

2 teaspoons distilled white or apple cider vinegar

3 tablespoons neutral oil, divided

3 cups fresh or frozen broccoli florets, thawed

1 small onion, chopped

1 pound 80/20 ground beef

Kosher salt

Freshly ground black pepper

Steamed white rice, for serving

In a medium bowl, whisk together the water, soy sauce, brown sugar, cornstarch, garlic, and vinegar until combined and the sugar has dissolved. Set aside.

Heat 1 tablespoon of the oil in a large nonstick skillet or wok over medium-high heat until shimmering. Add the broccoli and cook, stirring occasionally, until tender-crisp and blackened in spots, 6 to 7 minutes. Transfer the broccoli to a large bowl and set aside.

Reduce the heat to medium and add the remaining 2 tablespoons of oil to the skillet. Add the onion and cook until slightly translucent, 5 to 6 minutes. Add the ground beef and sprinkle with a pinch of salt and pepper. Cook, stirring occasionally to break the meat into crumbles, until browned, about 5 minutes. Add the sauce. Turn the heat up to medium-high and cook, stirring constantly, until the sauce thickens slightly, about 3 minutes. Fold in the cooked broccoli. Once the sauce has thickened, turn the heat off and serve with white rice or your choice of side.

Country Fried Steak *with* Brown Gravy

Serves 6 to 8

For the steaks

2 pounds cube steaks or boneless chuck steaks pounded to ¼-inch thick

1 teaspoon kosher salt

½ teaspoon freshly ground black pepper

2 cups all-purpose flour

2 tablespoons Miss Brown's House Seasoning (page 31)

1 cup whole milk

2 large eggs

Vegetable oil, for frying

For the gravy

1 medium yellow onion, sliced

Kosher salt

4 tablespoons (½ stick) unsalted butter

¼ cup all-purpose flour

2 cups water

Freshly ground black pepper

For serving

Mashed potatoes or rice

TO MAKE THE STEAKS:

Sprinkle the steaks with the salt and pepper. Combine the flour and House Seasoning in a shallow dish. Whisk together the milk and eggs in a separate shallow dish. Dredge the steaks in the flour mixture and shake off the excess. Dip the steaks in the milk mixture and then in the flour mixture again, pressing to coat well. Place the coated steaks on a rimmed baking sheet.

Pour enough oil into a large cast-iron skillet to reach 1 inch up the sides. Heat to medium-high heat (about 350°F).

Fry the steaks, in batches, until golden brown and crispy, 3 to 4 minutes. Drain on paper towels.

TO MAKE THE GRAVY:

Remove most of the oil from the pan but leave all of the crunchy bits at the bottom. That's the good stuff. Add the onion to the skillet and season with salt. Cook until the onions are slightly softened and translucent, 2 to 3 minutes. Add the butter and flour and cook until fragrant and browned, about 1 minute longer.

Gradually add the water, scraping up the browned bits from the bottom of the skillet with a wooden spoon. Simmer until the gravy is thickened, 3 to 4 minutes.

Taste and add salt and pepper to your liking.

TO SERVE:

Top the steaks with the gravy and serve with mashed potatoes or rice.

Lowcountry Low 'n' Slow Roast

Serves 6

- 3 pounds boneless beef chuck roast
- ½ cup yellow mustard
- 1 tablespoon Miss Brown's House Seasoning (page 31)
- 2 tablespoons neutral oil, plus more if needed
- 4 tablespoons (½ stick) unsalted butter
- 2 medium yellow onions, sliced
- 2 tablespoons tomato paste
- 1 15-ounce can stewed tomatoes
- 1 tablespoon Worcestershire sauce
- 2 teaspoons garlic powder
- 1 tablespoon sugar
- Kosher salt
- Freshly ground black pepper
- 2¼ cups beef broth, divided
- 4 medium carrots, peeled and chopped
- 3 celery ribs, washed and chopped
- 2 tablespoons all-purpose flour
- Mashed potatoes or rice, for serving

Preheat the oven to 325°F.

Dry the roast with paper towels, rub the yellow mustard on both sides, then generously season both sides with the House Seasoning. Place a Dutch oven on the stove over medium-high heat and add enough oil to cover the bottom of the pot, about 2 tablespoons. Once the oil is hot, carefully place the chuck roast into the oil and sear for 3 to 4 minutes, or until the roast has a good, brown crust. Flip with tongs and repeat on the other side, then remove the roast and place onto a plate.

Melt the butter in the Dutch oven, using a wooden spoon to scrape up the brown bits on the bottom. Add the onions, tomato paste, stewed tomatoes, Worcestershire sauce, garlic powder, sugar, and a pinch of salt and pepper and stir well. Cook for 3 minutes. Your house should smell amazing at this point. Slowly add 2 cups of the beef broth and whisk. Cook for another 3 to 4 minutes until the mixture comes to a slight boil. Taste and adjust the seasoning to your liking. Carefully add the roast, carrots, and celery to the pot. Put the lid on and cook in the preheated oven for 3 hours. Take the pot out of the oven, place it on the stove, and remove the roast. Using 2 forks, shred the meat on a plate. Cover with foil and set aside. In a small bowl, whisk together the remaining ¼ cup broth and the flour to make a slurry. Pour it into the pot and whisk over medium-high heat until a gravy forms. Turn the stove off. Top the roast with the gravy and serve over mashed potatoes or rice.

Grilled "Poke" Chops

Serves 4

- 2 tablespoons Miss Brown's House Seasoning (page 31)
- 1 tablespoon olive oil
- 1 tablespoon soy sauce
- 1 teaspoon yellow mustard
- 1 tablespoon packed light brown sugar
- 1 tablespoon apple cider vinegar
- 4 thin bone-in pork loin chops (about 2 pounds total)

In a small bowl, whisk together the House Seasoning, olive oil, soy sauce, mustard, brown sugar, and vinegar.

Put the pork chops in a baking dish or resealable gallon-size bag. Spread the marinade over the meat. Marinate for at least 1 hour at room temperature and up to 8 hours refrigerated.

Preheat an indoor grill pan or heavy-bottom skillet over medium heat.

Grill the pork chops until an instant-read thermometer inserted into the thickest part of the chops registers 145°F, 4 to 5 minutes per side. Let the meat rest for 3 to 4 minutes before serving with the side of your choice.

Grandma's Meatballs

Serves 6 to 8

- 1 cup day-old loaf bread torn into 1-inch pieces, or ½ cup plain breadcrumbs
- ¼ cup whole milk
- 1 pound 80/20 ground beef
- 1 pound ground pork sausage
- ½ cup grated Parmesan cheese
- 2 teaspoons Italian seasoning
- 1 teaspoon garlic powder
- Kosher salt
- Freshly ground black pepper
- 2 large eggs
- 2 24-ounce jars marinara sauce (I like Rao's)
- Cooked spaghetti or pasta of your choice, for serving

Preheat the oven to 400°F. Line a large rimmed baking sheet with parchment paper.

Combine the day-old bread and milk in a small bowl. Let stand until the liquid is absorbed, about 5 minutes.

Gently combine the bread mixture, beef, sausage, cheese, Italian seasoning, garlic powder, a pinch of salt and pepper, and eggs in a large bowl. Be careful not to overmix.

Use a small cookie scoop to shape the mixture into 1-inch balls (you should get 20 to 25 meatballs). Place them ½ inch apart on the prepared baking sheet. Bake until the meatballs are cooked through, about 20 minutes.

Meanwhile, heat the marinara sauce in a large Dutch oven over medium heat. Remove the cooked meatballs from the baking sheet and add to the simmering sauce. Serve with cooked spaghetti or pasta of your choice.

Honey-Glazed Pork Tenderloin Skillet Dinner

Serves 6

For the potatoes

2 pounds baby red potatoes, sliced in half
1 large sweet onion, sliced
2 apples, peeled, cored, and sliced (I prefer Gala or Fuji apples)
2 tablespoons neutral oil
2 teaspoons Italian seasoning
1 teaspoon kosher salt
1 teaspoon freshly ground black pepper

For the pork

½ cup honey
¼ cup neutral oil
¼ cup chicken broth
¼ cup apple juice
1 tablespoon Dijon mustard
Kosher salt
Freshly ground black pepper
2 pounds boneless pork loin

Preheat the oven to 400°F.

TO MAKE THE POTATOES:
Place the potatoes, onion, and apples in a 10- or 12-inch cast-iron skillet.

Add the oil, Italian seasoning, salt, and pepper; toss to combine. Bake for 25 minutes.

TO MAKE THE PORK:
While the potatoes are in the oven, whisk the honey, oil, chicken broth, apple juice, mustard, and a pinch of salt and pepper in a small bowl until thoroughly combined.

Brush the pork tenderloin with the honey mixture and place it over the potatoes. Pour any remaining honey mixture over the potatoes and pork.

Bake for an additional 22 to 25 minutes, or until the potatoes are tender and the tenderloin is cooked through. Pork is cooked through when the internal temperature registers at 145°F. Do *not* cook any longer or the pork will be dry.

Remove from the oven and let stand about 5 minutes before slicing and serving.

Ham *and* Cheese Bake

Serves 6 to 8

- 12 to 16 croissants, cut into large pieces (about 12 cups)
- 6 ounces cubed ham
- 8 ounces white cheddar cheese (or any sharp cheese you have on hand)
- 1½ cups half-and-half
- 6 large eggs
- 1 tablespoon Dijon mustard
- 2 teaspoons dried parsley flakes
- ½ teaspoon kosher salt
- ½ teaspoon freshly ground black pepper
- 4 tablespoons (½ stick) unsalted butter, melted and cooled

Preheat the oven to 350°F. Spray a 9 × 13-inch baking pan with nonstick spray.

Arrange the croissant pieces, ham, and cheese in the prepared baking pan. In a large bowl, mix the half-and-half, eggs, mustard, parsley, salt, pepper, and butter and pour over the ingredients in the pan. Give the mixture a slight toss and let it sit for 20 minutes. Cover with foil and bake for 30 minutes. Remove the foil and bake for another 10 to 15 minutes, or until the top is golden brown and the cheese is bubbling. Serve immediately.

Pork 'n' Beans (Poor Man's Meal)

Serves 6

- Neutral oil
- 3 hot dogs, sliced into rounds
- ½ medium yellow onion, finely diced
- 3 15-ounce cans baked beans (do not drain)
- ⅓ cup molasses or packed light brown sugar
- 1 tablespoon yellow mustard
- Pinch of freshly ground black pepper
- Pinch of Miss Brown's House Seasoning (page 31)
- Steamed white rice, for serving

Coat the bottom of a cast-iron skillet or a heavy-bottom pan with oil and place over medium heat. Add the hot dogs and sear, stirring occasionally, until the fat begins to render out, 3 to 4 minutes. Add the onion and cook, stirring occasionally, until the onion is translucent, 8 to 10 minutes.

Add the beans with their liquid, the molasses, mustard, and a pinch of ground pepper. Cook, stirring occasionally, until the flavors meld and the sauce thickens, 15 to 20 minutes. Taste and season with the House Seasoning. Serve with rice.

Bryon's Nachos

Serves 3 to 4

For the cheese sauce

2 tablespoons unsalted butter

2 tablespoons all-purpose flour

⅛ teaspoon cayenne pepper

1 cup milk

8 ounces cubed processed American cheese (or Velveeta® cheese)

Pinch of salt

For the nachos

1 pound 80/20 ground beef

1 tablespoon taco seasoning

1 10-ounce can Ro-Tel® tomatoes (do not drain)

1 9¼-ounce package Doritos® chips

Optional toppings

½ cup diced fresh tomatoes

2 tablespoons fresh cilantro, chopped

¼ cup pickled jalapeños

1 dollop sour cream

TO MAKE THE CHEESE SAUCE:

Melt the butter in a large saucepan over medium-high heat. Whisk in the flour and cayenne pepper and cook 1 to 2 minutes.

Whisk in the milk and bring to a simmer. Reduce the heat to low and add the cheese. Stir until the cheese is melted. Season with salt. Remove from the heat.

TO MAKE THE NACHOS:

Place a large, deep skillet over medium-high heat. Add the ground beef and cook for 5 to 6 minutes, breaking up the meat with a spatula or a wooden spoon as it cooks. Stir in the taco seasoning and cook for another 2 minutes or until the meat is cooked through and no pink is visible. Add the canned tomatoes and the cheese sauce to the pan with the beef. Stir and cook for 2 to 3 more minutes. Arrange the chips on a platter. Pour the beef and cheese dip over the chips; top with the fresh tomatoes, cilantro, jalapeños, and sour cream, if using, or other toppings of your choice.

Sausage *and* Grits

Serves 4

- 2 cups heavy cream
- 4 tablespoons (½ stick) unsalted butter
- 1 teaspoon kosher salt
- 1 teaspoon freshly ground black pepper
- 2 to 3 cups water, divided
- 1½ cups white grits (I like Marsh Hen Mill)
- 1 cup shredded sharp cheddar cheese, divided
- 1 tablespoon neutral oil
- 1 green bell pepper, sliced
- 1 red bell pepper, sliced
- 1 large white onion, sliced
- 12 ounces smoked sausage links, sliced into rounds
- 2 teaspoons Miss Brown's House Seasoning (page 31)
- 2 green onions, chopped, for garnish (optional)

Combine the heavy cream, butter, salt, pepper, and 2 cups of the water in a large saucepan. Whisk in the grits. Bring the mixture to a boil, whisking constantly. Reduce the heat to low and simmer, stirring occasionally, until the liquid is absorbed and the grits are creamy, about 30 minutes. If the grits are too thick, add additional water, up to 1 cup, until the grits are tender and to your liking. Stir in the cheddar cheese. Cover and keep on low heat while you cook the sausage.

Pour the oil into a large skillet over medium-high heat. Sauté the bell peppers and onion together until soft and lightly caramelized, 10 to 12 minutes. Stir in the sausage rounds and House Seasoning. Cook until the sausage becomes golden brown, 3 to 4 minutes. Turn the heat off and serve the sausage on top of the grits. Garnish with the green onions, if desired.

Hamburger Skillet

Serves 4

- 1 tablespoon vegetable oil
- 1 cup diced onion
- 2 cloves garlic, minced
- 1 pound 80/20 ground beef
- 1 tablespoon Miss Brown's House Seasoning (page 31)
- 1½ cups beef stock
- 2 tablespoons ketchup
- ½ tablespoon cornstarch
- 1 pound elbow macaroni, cooked according to package directions
- 6 ounces cubed American cheese (or 6 to 7 slices)
- Kosher salt
- Freshly ground black pepper
- 2 tablespoons green onions, chopped, for garnish (optional)

Heat the oil in a large cast-iron skillet over medium heat. Add the onion, garlic, ground beef, and House Seasoning. Cook until the onion begins to soften and the beef is slightly browned and no longer pink, about 7 minutes.

Stir in the beef stock, ketchup, and cornstarch, then increase the heat to medium-high and bring the mixture to a rolling boil. Reduce the heat to low and cook until the sauce reduces by half, 5 to 10 minutes. Add the prepared macaroni and continue to cook, stirring constantly, until the liquid starts to be slightly absorbed. Stir in the cheese. Remove from the heat and season with salt and pepper. Top with the green onions, if desired.

On-the-Run Breakfast Sandwich

Makes 6 sandwiches

- Unsalted butter or nonstick cooking spray
- 6 large eggs
- 1 tablespoon milk
- Kosher salt
- Freshly ground black pepper
- 6 English muffins or frozen biscuits
- 6 slices of American cheese (or whatever cheese you like)
- 6 precooked sausage patties or ham slices

Preheat the oven to 325°F. Grease an 8 × 8-inch baking dish with unsalted butter. Whisk the eggs, milk, pinch of salt, and pepper to taste. Pour the egg mixture into the greased pan and bake for 18 minutes, or just until the center is firm and set.

Remove the eggs from the oven and allow them to cool before cutting them into 6 pieces.

Top the bottom piece of each English muffin with egg, a slice of cheese, a sausage patty, and the other half of the muffin. Wrap each sandwich individually in parchment paper and place them in a freezer-safe bag. Freeze for up to 30 days.

The night before you need them, thaw the sandwiches in the fridge. Remove the parchment paper and wrap each sandwich in a slightly damp paper towel. Microwave each for 1 minute on the defrost setting. Flip the sandwich over and microwave for 10 to 30 seconds on high power, until warmed through. If you have a little more time, you can reheat the sandwiches in the toaster oven at 350°F for 10 to 12 minutes.

Minced Beef *and* Onion Pie

Serves 6

1 tablespoon neutral cooking oil

1½ pounds 80/20 ground beef

1 large onion, finely sliced

1 carrot, diced

2 stalks celery, sliced

1 clove garlic, minced

Kosher salt

Freshly ground black pepper

2 teaspoons dried herbs (Italian seasoning will do)

1 tablespoon all-purpose flour or cornstarch, plus additional flour for dusting

1 cup heavy whipping cream, half-and-half, or whole milk

¾ cup reduced-sodium beef broth

2 tablespoons Worcestershire sauce

1 large egg

1 tablespoon water

1 refrigerated piecrust, thawed

Preheat the oven to 400°F.

In a 10-inch cast-iron skillet over medium-high heat, add the oil and brown the ground beef with the onion, carrot, celery, and garlic. Season with heavy pinches of salt, pepper, and the dried herbs. Cook until the meat is no longer pink and the veggies have softened, about 5 minutes.

Lower the heat to medium and stir in the flour. Cook, stirring constantly, for 1 to 2 minutes. Stir in the cream, broth, and Worcestershire sauce. The mixture should thicken up a bit. Turn the burner off. In a small bowl, mix the egg and water. Place the piecrust on a floured surface and roll it out a bit more. Lay the piecrust over the beef mixture in the skillet. Crimp the edges or use the back of your fork to seal the piecrust to the skillet. Brush the top with the egg wash. Make a slit in the middle to allow air to escape. Bake for 35 to 40 minutes, or until golden brown.

Chef's note: You can make a double-crusted pie instead. Just remove the meat mixture from the skillet, wipe the skillet clean, and place a piecrust at the bottom. Pour the meat mixture back in and follow the directions above.

Sheet Pan Sausage *and* Squash

Serves 6 to 8

- 2 yellow squash, sliced into ¼-inch-thick rounds
- 2 zucchini, sliced into ¼-inch-thick rounds
- 1 small onion, cut into thin wedges
- 1 tablespoon olive oil
- Kosher salt
- Freshly ground black pepper
- ½ pound smoked pork sausage, sliced on a bias
- Rice or mashed potatoes, for serving

Preheat the oven to 400°F. Line a sheet pan with parchment paper.

Place the squash and zucchini in a large bowl with the onion. Add the oil, a pinch of salt, and a pinch of pepper. Toss the veggies to coat evenly and place them on the prepared sheet pan. Add the sliced sausage.

Roast for 25 to 30 minutes, or until the sausage is browned and the vegetables are tender. Serve with your favorite sides, such as rice or mashed potatoes.

Warm Potato Salad *with* Bacon

8 to 12 servings

4 slices thick-cut bacon

1 3-pound package fingerling potatoes (or a mix of baby potatoes)

Kosher salt

¾ cup extra-virgin olive oil

½ cup red wine vinegar

1 teaspoon honey

¼ cup whole-grain mustard

Freshly ground black pepper

2 cups baby arugula or spinach

½ cup chopped red onion

⅓ cup chopped fresh chives

Cook the bacon in a skillet, turning occasionally, until crisp, about 10 minutes. Remove from the skillet and crumble. Place the potatoes in a Dutch oven and cover with salted water. Bring to a boil and cook over medium-high heat until tender, about 25 minutes. Drain the potatoes and let cool completely, then cut them into bite-size pieces and transfer them to a serving bowl. In a medium bowl, whisk together the oil, vinegar, honey, and mustard. Season with salt and pepper. Add the arugula, onion, chives, and bacon to the potatoes. Pour the dressing over the potato mixture and toss gently to coat. Serve immediately or cover and refrigerate until ready to serve.

Mom's Lasagna Soup

Serves 6

- 1 tablespoon olive oil
- 1 medium white onion, diced
- 2 cloves garlic, minced
- ½ pound Italian sausage, casing removed
- 1 pound 80/20 ground beef
- 1 32-ounce container beef stock
- 2 15-ounce cans petite diced tomatoes
- 1 6-ounce can tomato paste
- ½ teaspoon dried oregano
- 8 uncooked lasagna noodles, broken into bite-size pieces
- ½ cup grated Parmesan cheese or shredded mozzarella
- Pinch of sugar
- Kosher salt
- Freshly ground black pepper
- Ricotta cheese, for serving
- Fresh parsley or basil (optional)

Heat the olive oil in a large pot or Dutch oven over medium heat. Add the onion and cook for 2 to 3 minutes. Stir in the garlic and cook 1 additional minute. Add the sausage and beef and cook until browned, using a wooden spoon to break the meat into smaller pieces. Add the stock, tomatoes, and tomato paste. Stir until combined and then add the oregano. When the soup comes to a light boil, add the noodles. Cook for 8 to 10 minutes, or until the noodles are tender. Stir in the cheese, sugar, and a little salt and pepper to taste. Ladle the soup into bowls and top each with a spoonful of ricotta cheese and fresh parsley or basil, if you have any on hand.

THREE

poultry perfected

CHICKEN HAS ALWAYS BEEN POPULAR and accessible. Nowadays, folks are eating more chicken than any other meat, twice as much as beef or pork.* Many people simply prefer to eat chicken over red meats for health reasons, and some are opting for poultry because it is usually budget friendly. In 2023, the average cost of a whole chicken was $1.92 per pound, compared to beef at between $4.95 and $10.75 per pound.**

Compared to cattle herding, chicken production has far lower cost barriers; chickens can be reared on small plots of land and mature quickly. And I'm a witness, cousins, to the ease of raising chickens. It was not uncommon in my grandmother's day to see neighbors who had chickens pecking around in their backyards.

Chicken breast can be very versatile, but it's generally pricey. However, you can prepare a lot of delicious meals with other, less expensive, parts—like thighs and wings. Cousins, you know me. I like to add some razzle-dazzle to the standards we know and love. Check out my Cajun Chicken Caesar Salad with Day-Old-Bread Croutons (page 78). And my "We Got McDonald's at Home" Chicken Nuggets (page 89) will satisfy the tastebuds of the young ones *and* the young at heart.

---

* Simone Melvin, "Americans Eat Twice as Much Chicken as Beef or Pork," *Forbes*, June 29, 2023, https://www.forbes.com/sites/simonemelvin/2023/06/29/americans-eat-twice-as-much-chicken-as-beef-or-pork-heres-why-it-will-take-a-while-for-lab-grown-meat-to-catch-up/.

** Melvin, "Americans Eat Twice as Much Chicken."

Carolina BBQ Baked Chicken

Serves 4

Nonstick cooking spray

For the Carolina BBQ sauce

1 cup yellow mustard

1 cup packed light brown sugar

½ cup granulated sugar

⅓ cup apple cider vinegar

1 tablespoon Worcestershire sauce

2 teaspoons hot sauce

For the chicken

1 whole fryer, cut into 8 pieces

2 teaspoons Miss Brown's House Seasoning (page 31)

Preheat the oven to 375°F. Line a rimmed baking sheet with aluminum foil and place a wire rack on top. Coat the rack with nonstick cooking spray.

TO MAKE THE CAROLINA BBQ SAUCE:
In a medium saucepan over medium heat, whisk together the mustard, brown sugar, granulated sugar, vinegar, Worcestershire sauce, and hot sauce. Simmer, stirring frequently, until the sauce thickens and the sugars dissolve, about 10 minutes. Set aside.

TO MAKE THE CHICKEN:
Pat the chicken dry with paper towels. Coat the chicken in House Seasoning on all sides. Place on the prepared baking sheet and bake for 45 minutes. Take the chicken out of the oven. In a large bowl, toss the chicken with ½ cup of the Carolina BBQ sauce. Place the chicken back on the baking sheet and bake for another 15 minutes, until the chicken has browned/caramelized and a thermometer registers 165°F.

Brush the chicken with more sauce before serving. Use as much sauce as you like.

Country Skillet Potpie

Serves 8

- 1 tablespoon vegetable oil
- 8 tablespoons (1 stick) unsalted butter, divided
- 1 stalk celery, diced
- ½ large yellow onion, diced
- Kosher salt
- 1 clove garlic, minced
- 1 cup frozen peas and carrots, thawed
- ¼ cup all-purpose flour
- 1½ cups chicken broth
- ½ cup whole milk
- Freshly ground black pepper
- 2½ cups diced cooked chicken
- 8 refrigerated biscuits (or 8 frozen biscuits, thawed)
- 1 large egg
- 1 tablespoon water

Preheat the oven to 400°F.

Heat the oil and 6 tablespoons of the butter in a large oven-safe pan or cast-iron skillet over medium-high heat. Add the celery, onion, and a heavy pinch of salt and cook until the vegetables are soft and the onions turn translucent, about 10 minutes. Add the garlic and sauté for 1 minute, then stir in the peas and carrots. Add the flour and cook, stirring constantly, about 2 minutes. Slowly add the chicken broth and milk, whisking to remove any flour lumps. Bring to a simmer and cook until thickened, about 5 minutes. Season with salt and pepper. Add the chicken and stir to combine. Top with the biscuits. In a small bowl, beat together the egg and water, then brush the egg wash over the biscuits.

Bake until the biscuits are a deep golden brown and the filling is bubbly, 20 to 25 minutes. Let cool slightly before serving. Top with the remaining 2 tablespoons of butter right before serving.

Hot Honey Drumsticks

Serves 6

For the chicken

1 cup all-purpose flour

1 tablespoon Miss Brown's House Seasoning (page 31)

¾ cup milk

1 large egg

Kosher salt

Freshly ground black pepper

2 pounds chicken drumsticks

Enough oil for deep frying

For the hot honey sauce

6 tablespoons (¾ stick) unsalted butter

½ cup honey

¼ cup hot sauce

1 teaspoon cayenne pepper

½ teaspoon chili powder

½ teaspoon smoked paprika

½ teaspoon garlic powder

Pinch of sea salt

TO MAKE THE CHICKEN:

Combine the flour with the House Seasoning and set aside.

Whisk together the milk, egg, pinch of salt, and pepper to taste in a separate bowl and set aside. Dip each chicken piece in the seasoned flour, then in the egg mixture, and then back into the flour.

Heat the oil to 350°F in a Dutch oven and place the drumsticks carefully in the oil. Fry for 13 to 15 minutes until golden brown and the internal temperature reaches 165°F. Remove the Dutch oven from the heat and transfer the chicken to a wire rack on top of a sheet pan.

TO MAKE THE HOT HONEY SAUCE:

In a medium saucepan over medium-high heat, combine the butter, honey, hot sauce, cayenne pepper, chili powder, smoked paprika, garlic powder, and sea salt. Cook until the ingredients come together and the sauce becomes smooth and thick, 3 to 4 minutes.

Toss the chicken with the sauce, or drizzle the sauce on top of the chicken. Serve warm.

Cajun Chicken Caesar Salad *with* Day-Old-Bread Croutons

Serves 4

For the croutons

3 tablespoons neutral oil

1 teaspoon garlic powder

Kosher salt

Freshly ground black pepper

4 cups day-old white bread cubes

For the chicken

3 tablespoons neutral oil

2 tablespoons freshly squeezed lemon juice

2 teaspoons lemon zest

1 clove garlic, minced

1 tablespoon Cajun seasoning

1½ pounds boneless, skinless chicken thighs

For the salad

1 large head Romaine lettuce (or lettuce of your choice)

½ cup Caesar dressing

⅓ cup grated or shaved Parmesan cheese

TO MAKE THE CROUTONS:

Preheat the oven to 400°F.

In a small bowl, whisk together the oil, garlic powder, and salt and pepper to taste. Spread the bread cubes in a single layer on a baking sheet. Toss the bread with the oil mixture to coat. Bake until golden brown, 12 to 13 minutes; set aside.

TO MAKE THE CHICKEN:

In a medium bowl, combine the oil, lemon juice, lemon zest, garlic, and Cajun seasoning. Add the chicken and marinate at least 2 hours or overnight.

When ready to prepare, preheat a grill or frying pan to medium-high heat. Remove the chicken from the marinade and cook, turning occasionally, until the chicken is completely cooked through, reaching an internal temperature of 165°F, 4 to 5 minutes per side. Let the chicken cool before dicing it into bite-size pieces.

TO MAKE THE SALAD:

Place the lettuce in a large bowl; top with the chicken and croutons. Pour the dressing on top of the salad and toss gently to combine. Top with the Parmesan.

Ramen Chicken Noddle Soup

Serves 4

1 tablespoon olive oil
1 medium yellow onion, finely diced
1 stalk celery, finely diced
1 tablespoon concentrated chicken base, such as Better Than Bouillon
1 teaspoon Italian seasoning
Heavy pinch of garlic powder
Heavy pinch of onion powder
5 cups water
Kosher salt
Freshly ground black pepper
1½ cups skinned shredded rotisserie chicken
1½ cups frozen mixed vegetables
1 3-ounce package ramen noodles, broken into pieces
⅓ cup chopped fresh parsley, plus more for garnish

Heat the oil in a Dutch oven over medium-high heat. Add the onion and celery and cook until softened, about 5 minutes. Stir in the bouillon, Italian seasoning, garlic powder, and onion powder and cook until fragrant, about 1 minute.

Gradually add 5 cups of water and stir until combined. Season with salt and pepper. Bring to a boil. Stir in the chicken, vegetables, noodles, and parsley. Simmer until the noodles are tender, about 7 minutes. Spoon the soup into bowls and garnish with additional fresh parsley.

Lowcountry Chicken Bog

Serves 6

- 1 whole fryer chicken (about 4 pounds), cut into 8 pieces, skin removed
- Salt
- Freshly ground black pepper
- Neutral cooking oil
- 1 pound smoked sausage, sliced on a bias
- 4 tablespoons (½ stick) unsalted butter
- 1 large white or yellow onion, diced
- 1 stalk celery, finely diced
- 1 small green bell pepper, diced
- 2 cups medium-grain rice
- Water
- 3 tablespoons chopped green onion, for garnish (optional)
- 3 tablespoons chopped fresh parsley, for garnish (optional)

Season the chicken with salt and pepper.

In a Dutch oven over medium-high heat, add enough oil to cover the bottom of the pot. Add 4 pieces of chicken. Cook until golden brown on both sides and cooked all the way through, 5 to 6 minutes per side. Remove the first batch of chicken, then repeat with the remaining pieces. Place the chicken on a plate and shred.

In the same pot, sauté the sausage until browned, 5 to 6 minutes. Remove with a slotted spoon. Melt the butter in the same pot, then add the onion, celery, and bell pepper. Sprinkle with a little salt and cook until the vegetables turn translucent, 5 to 7 minutes. Add the rice and shredded chicken and stir to combine. Cook for about 2 minutes, stirring often. Add the smoked sausage and enough water to cover the rice. Add a pinch or two of salt and pepper. Stir gently, then cover the pot and turn the heat to low. Cook gently until the rice is done, 15 to 20 minutes. Uncover and fluff before garnishing with green onion and parsley, if desired.

Smothered Turkey Wings

Serves 4

For the turkey wings

- 3 to 4 pounds turkey wings, split into flats and drumsticks
- 3 tablespoons neutral oil
- 3 tablespoons Miss Brown's House Seasoning (page 31)
- Salt
- Freshly ground black pepper
- 2 teaspoons poultry seasoning
- 2 tablespoons unsalted butter

For the gravy

- 2 tablespoons unsalted butter
- 1 large yellow onion, thinly sliced
- 1 large green bell pepper, sliced
- 2 cloves garlic, minced
- ⅛ teaspoon poultry seasoning
- ¼ teaspoon paprika
- ¼ cup all-purpose flour
- 2 cups chicken stock, room temperature
- Salt
- Freshly ground black pepper

TO MAKE THE TURKEY WINGS:
Preheat the oven to 350°F.

Place the turkey wings in a large bowl, drizzle with the oil, then sprinkle with the House Seasoning, a heavy pinch of salt, a heavy pinch of pepper, and the poultry seasoning, coating the wings on both sides.

In a large skillet, preferably cast-iron, over medium-high heat, melt the butter. Working in batches, making sure not to overcrowd the pan, sear the turkey wings until golden brown on both sides. Once seared, remove the wings to a 9 × 13-inch baking dish. Leave the drippings in the skillet.

TO MAKE THE GRAVY:
To the same skillet, add the butter, onion, bell pepper, and garlic. Cook until the veggies have softened, then stir in the poultry seasoning, paprika, and flour. Cook for 1 to 2 more minutes. Whisk in the stock. Let the mixture simmer for 3 to 4 minutes until it thickens. Taste and add salt and pepper to your liking.

Pour the gravy over the wings. It will thicken more in the oven. Cover the pan and bake the wings for 1 hour. Then uncover, baste, and crank the oven temperature up to 375°F. Roast for 35 to 40 minutes or until golden brown and bubbling. I like to serve the wings over white rice.

Brown Sugar-Glazed Chicken Thighs

Serves 4 to 6

3 pounds bone-in chicken thighs
Salt
Freshly ground black pepper
Neutral cooking oil
½ cup packed dark brown sugar
8 cloves garlic, minced
2 tablespoons white vinegar
¼ cup soy sauce
¼ cup chicken broth
½ teaspoon ground ginger

Preheat the oven to 350°F.

Pat the chicken thighs dry with a paper towel. Season with a few pinches of salt and pepper.

In a 10-inch cast-iron or oven-safe skillet over medium-high heat, add a drizzle of the neutral oil and sear both sides of the chicken thighs until the skin turns slightly golden brown.

While the chicken is browning, whisk the brown sugar, garlic, vinegar, soy sauce, broth, ginger, and salt and pepper to taste in a small saucepan over medium heat until the sugar dissolves, about 5 to 6 minutes.

Turn off the heat under the chicken. Arrange the chicken skin side up and pour the sauce over it. Bake uncovered for 30 minutes, basting with the sauce every 10 minutes. Serve warm with your favorite sides.

Lemon Pepper Roasted Chicken Wings

Serves 4

- 2 pounds whole chicken wings or wingettes
- 3 tablespoons olive oil
- Zest of 1 lemon
- Juice of 1 lemon (about 2 tablespoons)
- ½ tablespoon lemon pepper seasoning
- 1 teaspoon Italian seasoning
- 1 teaspoon garlic powder
- ¼ teaspoon salt
- 6 tablespoons (¾ stick) unsalted butter, melted

Pat the chicken wings dry with a paper towel. In a small bowl, combine the oil, lemon zest, lemon juice, lemon pepper seasoning, Italian seasoning, garlic powder, and salt. Place the wings and the marinade in a plastic zip-top bag. Marinate for at least 2 hours or overnight in the fridge.

When ready to cook, preheat the oven to 450°F. Allow the wings to sit out during this time to come to room temperature. Remove the marinated chicken from the bag, reserving any leftover marinade, and place it in a single layer in a 9 × 13-inch baking dish. Pour the melted butter and reserved marinade over the chicken. Bake for 30 to 45 minutes, or until the chicken is fully cooked and golden brown and the internal temperature reads at least 165°F. Remove the chicken wings from the oven and enjoy with the sides of your choice.

"We Got McDonald's *at* Home" Chicken Nuggets

Makes 30 nuggets

- Enough oil to deep fry
- 2 pounds ground chicken breast
- 2 large eggs
- 2 tablespoons Miss Brown's House Seasoning, divided (page 31)
- 1 cup all-purpose flour, divided
- 1 cup cornstarch
- 1 cup water

Add the oil to about halfway in a Dutch oven and heat to 350°F. Line a baking sheet with parchment paper.

In a large bowl, mix the ground chicken with the eggs and 1 tablespoon of the House Seasoning. Set aside.

Place ¼ cup of the flour into a shallow bowl. Form the chicken into small, nugget-size patties, then dredge both sides in the flour. Set the nuggets on the prepared baking sheet.

In a medium bowl, combine the remaining ¾ cup of flour, the cornstarch, and the remaining 1 tablespoon of House Seasoning. Add the water and stir until the batter is blended completely. Dip a chicken nugget into the batter, shake off the excess, and carefully lower the nugget into the hot oil. Repeat with the remaining nuggets. Cook, flipping with tongs once or twice until golden brown on both sides and completely cooked on the inside. Drain on a paper towel–lined plate. Serve with your favorite dipping sauces.

Grilled Alabama Chicken

Serves 3

For the chicken

- 3 tablespoons Miss Brown's House Seasoning (page 31)
- 2 tablespoons packed light brown sugar
- 1 teaspoon oregano
- 1 teaspoon smoked paprika
- 1 teaspoon dried parsley
- Kosher salt
- Freshly ground black pepper
- 3 chicken quarters, fat trimmed

For the Alabama white sauce

- 1 cup mayonnaise
- 2 tablespoons packed light brown sugar
- 2 tablespoons apple cider vinegar
- 1 tablespoon Dijon mustard
- 2 teaspoons hot sauce
- Juice of ½ lemon (about 1 tablespoon)
- Kosher salt
- Freshly ground black pepper

TO MAKE THE CHICKEN:

In a small bowl, stir together the House Seasoning, brown sugar, oregano, paprika, parsley, and a couple of pinches of salt and ground black pepper. Rub the mixture all over the chicken quarters and under the skin.

Prepare a grill for direct and indirect cooking: Heat one side of the grill to medium heat; leave the other side unlit. Place the chicken quarters skin side up on the grates on the unlit side of the grill. Grill, with the lid closed, until the skin begins to brown, about 45 minutes. Transfer the chicken to the lit side of the grill, skin side up, and cook 12 to 15 minutes on each side until the chicken is done and a meat thermometer registers 165°F when inserted into the thickest portion of the thigh (avoiding bone).

TO MAKE THE ALABAMA WHITE SAUCE:

In a medium bowl, stir together the mayonnaise, brown sugar, vinegar, Dijon mustard, hot sauce, lemon juice, and salt and pepper to taste.

Transfer the chicken to a serving platter. Pour the sauce over the chicken and serve immediately.

Blackened Chicken Pasta

Serves 4

12 ounces spaghetti

Kosher salt

8 tablespoons (1 stick) unsalted butter, divided

1 pound boneless, skinless chicken breast, sliced into strips

1½ tablespoons Cajun seasoning, divided

12 ounces andouille sausage, sliced

1 small yellow onion, diced

1 large green bell pepper, diced

4 cloves garlic, minced

1 large beefsteak tomato, diced

1½ cups heavy cream or whole milk

1 teaspoon lemon juice

⅓ cup grated Parmesan cheese, plus more for topping

1 tablespoon chopped fresh parsley

Freshly ground black pepper

4 green onions, sliced (optional)

Cook the spaghetti in salted water according to package directions. Drain, reserving about ¼ cup of the starchy pasta water.

While cooking the spaghetti, melt 2 tablespoons of the butter in a large skillet over medium-high heat. Season the chicken with half of the Cajun seasoning and cook it with the sausage in the butter until the chicken has cooked through and the sausage has browned, 8 to 10 minutes.

Remove the chicken and sausage with a slotted spoon and set aside.

Add the remaining 6 tablespoons of butter to the skillet. When melted, add the onion and bell pepper and cook until the veggies are soft, 6 to 7 minutes.

Stir in the garlic and tomato and cook 1 minute.

Stir in the heavy cream, reserved pasta water, and remaining Cajun seasoning and simmer until thickened a bit.

Add the lemon juice, Parmesan, and parsley. Stir to melt the cheese.

Check for seasoning and add salt and pepper to taste.

Remove from the heat. Add the pasta, chicken, and sausage to the skillet, and mix in. Top with more Parmesan and the green onions, if desired.

Homemade Chicken Stock

Makes about 10 cups

- 1 5- to 6-pound whole, fresh chicken, quartered (reserve the chicken back)
- 1 large yellow onion, chopped
- 2 carrots, halved
- 3 stalks celery, halved
- 6 sprigs fresh parsley
- 5 sprigs fresh thyme
- 1 head garlic, unpeeled, halved crosswise
- 1 tablespoon salt
- 2 teaspoons freshly ground black pepper
- 12 cups water

In a large stock pot, place the chicken (including the back), onion, carrots, celery, parsley, thyme, garlic, salt, and pepper. Add the water and bring to a boil over medium-high heat. Reduce the heat to low and allow to simmer uncovered for 2 hours. Remove the chicken, herbs, and veggies. With a sieve, strain the broth into a large bowl. Cover the bowl with plastic wrap and refrigerate for at least 6 hours. The fat will separate and rise to the top, where it can be removed with a spoon.

Store the broth in airtight containers or mason jars in the refrigerator for up to 5 days or in the freezer in freezer-safe containers for at least 3 months.

Southern-Style Stewed Chicken

Serves 4

- ¾ cup neutral cooking oil, divided
- 3- to 4-pound whole fryer chicken, cut into 8 pieces
- Salt
- Freshly ground black pepper
- 1 tablespoon Miss Brown's House Seasoning (page 31)
- ½ cup all-purpose flour
- 1 large yellow onion, diced
- 1 bell pepper, diced
- 1 stalk celery, diced
- 2 quarts chicken stock
- 2 cloves garlic, minced
- Steamed white rice, for serving

Heat ¼ cup of the oil in a cast-iron or heavy-bottom Dutch oven over medium-high heat.

Season the chicken pieces on both sides with a few pinches of salt, pepper, and House Seasoning. Cooking in batches, brown the chicken, 5 to 6 minutes on each side; remove from the pot and set aside.

Add the remaining ½ cup of oil to the pot with the drippings. The oil should be enough to cover the bottom of the pot. Slowly whisk the flour in, a little at a time. Cook until the flour is incorporated and no lumps remain, 4 to 5 minutes, stirring regularly and scraping up the bits from the bottom of the pot. Add the onion, bell pepper, and celery and cook for 3 additional minutes until the roux becomes golden brown. Now begin adding in the stock, 1 cup at a time, constantly whisking until well incorporated.

Bring the mixture to a boil, reduce the heat to a low simmer, return the chicken to the pot, and simmer uncovered for 1 hour. Add the garlic and cook another 30 minutes. Taste for seasonings and add additional salt, pepper, or House Seasoning as needed. Serve over steamed white rice.

Chicken *and* Sausage Jambalaya

Serves 4

- ¼ cup vegetable oil, divided, plus more as needed
- ½ pound andouille sausage, sliced into half-moons
- 1 pound boneless, skinless chicken breast, cut into ½-inch cubes
- Kosher salt
- Freshly ground black pepper
- ½ large white onion, diced
- ½ cup green bell pepper, diced
- ½ cup celery, diced
- 1 tablespoon Cajun seasoning
- 2 tablespoons unsalted butter
- 1½ cups medium-grain white rice
- 2 bay leaves
- 1½ cups chicken stock
- 1½ cups water
- ½ cup chopped green onions, sliced

Heat 2 tablespoons of the oil in a large Dutch oven over medium-high heat. Add the sausage and cook until it begins to brown, about 4 minutes. Remove to a large plate. Season the chicken with salt and pepper and add it to the skillet. Cook until golden brown, then remove it with a slotted spoon to the plate with the sausage.

Add a little more oil to the skillet. Add the onion, bell pepper, celery, Cajun seasoning, and salt to taste. Cook until the vegetables are tender, 8 to 10 minutes, stirring in the remaining 2 tablespoons of oil if needed. Add the butter and rice, and cook until the rice grains are coated, about 1 minute. Add the bay leaves, sausage, chicken, stock, and water to the pan; bring to a boil and stir. Cover, reduce the heat, and simmer until the liquid is absorbed and the rice is fluffy, 25 to 30 minutes. Remove the bay leaves, fold in the green onions, and serve.

Creamy Chicken *and* Rice Bake

Serves 4

- Nonstick cooking spray
- 3 10.5-ounce cans condensed cream of chicken soup (or cream of mushroom)
- 1 cup water
- 1 cup reduced-sodium chicken broth
- 2 cups dry parboiled rice
- 2 teaspoons Miss Brown's House Seasoning (page 31)
- 2 cups frozen vegetables, thawed
- 3 cups shredded rotisserie chicken
- 2 cups shredded yellow cheddar cheese (or any shredded cheese you have on hand)

Preheat the oven to 375°F. Spray a 9 × 13-inch baking dish with nonstick spray.

To the prepared baking dish, add the soup, water, broth, rice, and House Seasoning. Stir in the vegetables and chicken, then cover tightly with foil. Bake for about 45 minutes. Remove the dish from the oven and sprinkle the cheese on top. Return the dish to the oven uncovered, and bake for an additional 10 minutes or until the top is bubbly and golden brown.

Chicken Mafé

Serves 6 to 8

- 2 tablespoons neutral oil
- 1 large fryer chicken, cut into stewing pieces
- Kosher salt
- Freshly ground black pepper
- 1 large onion, diced
- 4 cloves garlic, minced
- 2 chicken bouillon cubes or 1 tablespoon of Better Than Bouillon
- One 14.5-ounce can tomato sauce
- 1 teaspoon tomato paste
- 1½ cups all-natural peanut butter
- 4 cups water
- 2 large sweet potatoes, peeled and cut into 1-inch pieces
- 1 5-ounce bag of fresh baby spinach (optional)
- Steamed white rice, for serving (optional)

Heat the oil in a large Dutch oven until hot. Sprinkle the chicken pieces with salt and pepper and cook until browned on all sides, about 20 minutes. Remove the chicken to a plate. Add the onion, garlic, and bouillon cubes to the pot and cook until the onion is translucent, about 5 minutes.

Stir in the tomato sauce, tomato paste, and peanut butter. Add the water and return the chicken to the pot. Bring to a boil; reduce the heat and let simmer for 10 to 12 minutes.

Add the sweet potatoes and spinach, if using. Cover and simmer until the potatoes are easily pierced with a fork, about 25 minutes. Serve warm with hot steamed rice, if desired.

Chicken *and* Sausage Gumbo

Serves 6

- ½ cup plus 2 tablespoons canola oil, divided
- 1 pound boneless chicken thighs
- Kosher salt
- Freshly ground black pepper
- 1 pound andouille sausage, sliced into ½-inch rounds
- ½ cup all-purpose flour
- 1 large yellow onion, chopped
- 2 stalks celery, chopped
- 1 large red bell pepper, chopped
- 2 to 3 tablespoons roasted chicken base, preferably Better Than Bouillon Roasted Chicken
- 2 cloves garlic, minced
- 1 tablespoon gumbo filé powder
- Pinch of Cajun seasoning
- 2 bay leaves
- 8 cups water
- 2 tablespoons chopped fresh parsley leaves, plus additional for topping
- 2 stalks green onion, chopped, plus additional for topping
- Steamed long-grain white rice, for serving

Heat 2 tablespoons of the oil in a large Dutch oven over medium-high heat. Sprinkle the chicken with salt and pepper, then sear until golden brown, 4 to 5 minutes per side. Remove the chicken from the pan and add the andouille sausage, cooking until golden brown, 5 to 6 minutes. Remove the sausage from the Dutch oven and set aside.

Combine the remaining ½ cup of oil and the flour in the Dutch oven and reduce the heat to medium. Cook, stirring continuously, to make a dark brown roux, 20 to 25 minutes. Add the onion, celery, bell pepper, and salt to taste. Cook, stirring, until the onions become transparent, 4 to 5 minutes. Add the chicken base, garlic, gumbo filé, Cajun seasoning, bay leaves, and additional salt and pepper. Cook, stirring, for another 2 to 3 minutes. Add the water to the pot. Using a large whisk, whisk until the roux mixture and the water are well combined. Bring to a boil, then reduce the heat to medium-low. Cook, uncovered and stirring occasionally, for 1 hour.

Turn the heat up to medium and return the chicken and sausage to the pot. Cover and simmer for 2 hours. Remove the pot from the heat. Fluff and gently stir in the parsley and scallions and remove the bay leaves. Garnish with additional parsley and scallions. Serve with white rice.

Turkey Smash Burgers

Serves 2

For the caramelized onions

2 tablespoons unsalted butter
1 large sweet yellow onion, thinly sliced
Kosher salt
1 tablespoon apple cider vinegar
Pinch of light brown sugar

For the Dijonnaise

2 tablespoons mayonnaise
2 tablespoons Dijon mustard
1 tablespoon Worcestershire sauce

For the smash burgers

1 pound ground turkey
¼ teaspoon kosher salt
¼ teaspoon freshly ground black pepper
1 tablespoon neutral oil
4 slices American cheese
2 hamburger buns or 4 slices of bread
Butter (optional)
1 cup shredded lettuce
Hamburger condiments (optional)

TO MAKE THE CARAMELIZED ONIONS:
Add the butter to a cast-iron or heavy-bottom skillet over medium heat. Once the butter has melted, add the onion and a pinch of salt. Cover and let the onion cook for 5 minutes undisturbed. As the onion cooks, it will begin to sweat, which creates steam in the pan. Remove the lid, add the Worcestershire sauce, apple cider vinegar, and brown sugar. Stir and cook for 2 to 3 more minutes. Transfer the onion to a plate and set aside.

TO MAKE THE DIJONNAISE:
In a small bowl, combine mayonnaise and Dijon and mix until combined. Set aside.

TO MAKE THE SMASH BURGERS:
Shape the turkey into 4 balls, about 4 ounces each. Sprinkle with salt and pepper. Adjust the heat under the cast-iron skillet to medium-high. When the pan is really hot, add the oil. Place the turkey balls, in batches if necessary, in the hot skillet and smash into flat discs with a burger press. (Smash each for about 10 seconds.)

Cook for 2 minutes, sprinkle with more salt and pepper, then flip. Cook until the patties are caramelized and browned, 1 to 2 minutes longer. Add the cheese and let stand until melted. Remove the patties from the skillet. If you'd like, toast the buns now with a little butter.

To assemble, spread the Dijonnaise on the buns. Top two bun halves with the shredded lettuce, 2 meat patties, onions, and any additional toppings of your choice. Place the remaining bun halves on top and serve.

FOUR

from sea to table

NATURALLY, THE GULLAH REGION—right off the Atlantic—is overflowing with great seafood options. Trust me, cousins, I know I was blessed to grow up with easy and relatively inexpensive access to all the *fish* and *shrimp* I could eat.

Of course, folks in the inland areas are not as fortunate. Frozen shrimp and other seafood work just as well as fresh in most of my recipes. And when I think about some of the most memorable fish dinners I had growing up, I realize we relied heavily on canned goods. What we are *not* going to do is throw shade on canned tuna and salmon. Both are not only nutritious—with more omega-3 fatty acids than many other options—but also affordable. Am I the only one here who remembers ShopRite's Can Can promotions? Whew, the deals!

No matter where you shop, use those kinds of sales to stock up. You simply can't go wrong with canned goods, and what's more is that their shelf life could almost take you into the next lifetime! Tuna melts are one of my all-time favorite comfort foods, and I love that they can be a filling lunch or a hearty dinner. And don't even get me started on my Canned Salmon Hash (page 116). Cousins, I'm here to tell you that canned fish can do no wrong.

Air Fryer Fish Sticks

Serves 2 to 3

For the tartar sauce

- 1 cup mayonnaise
- 2 to 3 tablespoons chopped dill pickles
- 1 tablespoon capers
- 1 tablespoon freshly squeezed lemon juice
- 2 teaspoons fresh dill (optional)
- 1 teaspoon sugar
- Kosher salt
- Freshly ground black pepper

For the fish sticks

- 1½ pounds cod fillets, or another meaty white fish like halibut
- Kosher salt
- Freshly ground black pepper
- 1 cup all-purpose flour
- 2 large eggs, beaten
- 1 cup panko breadcrumbs
- 3 teaspoons Miss Brown's House Seasoning (page 31)
- Nonstick cooking spray
- Zest of 1 lemon, for garnish

TO MAKE THE TARTAR SAUCE:

In a medium bowl, mix the mayonnaise, pickles, capers, lemon juice, dill (if using), and sugar. Season with salt and pepper.

TO MAKE THE FISH STICKS:

Preheat the air fryer to 375°F.

With paper towels, gently pat the cod fillets to draw out moisture; season them with salt and pepper.

Cut the fish into strips that measure about ½ inch wide and 3 to 4 inches long.

Place the flour, eggs, and breadcrumbs into separate shallow bowls to set up a dredging station assembly line. Mix the House Seasoning into the breadcrumbs. Dredge the fish sticks, one at a time, in the flour, eggs, and breadcrumbs. Spray the air fryer tray and the fish sticks with nonstick cooking spray. Now place the fish sticks in the basket, but be sure not to overcrowd them. Cook in batches if necessary. Cook the fish sticks for 3 minutes, then carefully flip them over using tongs, spray with a little more nonstick spray, and cook them for an additional 3 minutes. Once the batches are done, garnish the fish sticks with the lemon zest and serve with the tartar sauce.

Tuna Pasta Salad

Serves 8 to 10

- 12 ounces tricolor bow-tie pasta
- 1 stalk celery, cut into large chunks
- ½ red bell pepper
- ½ red onion
- 3 5-ounce cans solid white tuna in water, drained
- 3 large hard-boiled eggs, peeled and chopped
- ½ cup mayonnaise
- 1 tablespoon Dijon mustard
- 1 tablespoon white vinegar
- 2 teaspoons Miss Brown's House Seasoning (page 31)
- ½ cup sweet pickle relish
- Kosher salt
- Freshly ground black pepper
- Fresh curly parsley, chopped, for garnish (optional)

Cook the pasta in salted boiling water according to the package directions. Drain and run under cold water to cool, then drain again. Transfer the cooked pasta to a large serving bowl.

While the pasta cooks, pulse the celery, bell pepper, and onion in a food processor until finely minced. Add the vegetables, tuna, and eggs to the serving bowl with the pasta. Make sure to break up the tuna with a fork.

In a small bowl, stir together the mayonnaise, mustard, vinegar, House Seasoning, and relish. Pour the dressing over the pasta salad and toss gently to combine. Season with salt and pepper to taste. Garnish with the parsley before serving, if desired.

Zesty Italian Baked Salmon

Serves 4

Nonstick cooking spray

Kosher salt

Freshly ground black pepper

4 6-ounce salmon fillets

½ cup Italian dressing of your choice (I like Ken's Simply Vinaigrette)

Juice of 1 large lemon

Zest of 1 large lemon

1 cup grated Parmesan cheese, divided

1 pint cherry tomatoes

Preheat the oven to 400°F. Spray a 9 × 13-inch baking dish with nonstick cooking spray.

Sprinkle a pinch of salt and pepper on top of the salmon. Place the salmon fillets in the prepared baking dish. In a small bowl, combine the Italian dressing, lemon juice, lemon zest, and ½ cup of the Parmesan cheese. Pour the mixture over the salmon. Scatter the cherry tomatoes around the dish.

Bake for 12 to 15 minutes, or until the salmon is cooked through. The center should be opaque and flake easily with a fork. If the pieces are thick, the salmon may need to cook a few minutes longer.

Remove the salmon from the oven. Sprinkle with the remaining ½ cup of Parmesan and serve.

Canned Salmon Hash

Serves 4 to 6

- Kosher salt
- 1½ pounds white or Yukon Gold potatoes, peeled and diced into ½-inch pieces
- 4 slices bacon
- 1 tablespoon canola or any neutral oil
- 1 medium sweet yellow onion, diced
- 1 medium green bell pepper, diced
- 1 14-ounce can salmon, drained
- Freshly ground black pepper

Bring a large saucepan of salted water to a boil over high heat. Add the diced potatoes and cook until just tender, 6 to 8 minutes. Drain and set aside. Place the bacon in a 10- to 12-inch heavy-bottom skillet, preferably cast-iron. Cook until the bacon is crispy and the fat has rendered. Remove the bacon, leaving the rendered fat in the pan. Add the canola oil, onion, and bell pepper and sprinkle with a pinch of salt. Stir frequently until the veggies have slightly softened. Add the salmon and scramble with the sautéed veggies, then gently fold in the cooked potatoes. Sprinkle with a little salt and pepper to your taste. Let cook for 4 minutes undisturbed to create a crust, then gently stir and serve.

Lemon Pepper Fried Catfish

Serves 6

- 6 catfish fillets, about 1½ pounds
- 1 teaspoon kosher salt, plus more for sprinkling
- 1 teaspoon freshly ground black pepper, plus more for sprinkling
- 1 cup buttermilk
- 1½ cups yellow cornmeal
- ½ cup all-purpose flour
- 1 tablespoon lemon pepper seasoning
- Neutral cooking oil, for frying
- 1 lemon, halved

Sprinkle the catfish fillets with kosher salt and ground black pepper on both sides. Place the seasoned fillets in a shallow dish or resealable bag and cover with the buttermilk, turning to coat. Set aside to soak while preparing the rest of the ingredients, or move to the fridge to marinate for up to 8 hours.

Combine the cornmeal, flour, and lemon pepper seasoning in a paper bag or a zip-top bag. Toss to evenly disperse the spices. Heat ½ to 1 inch of oil in a 10-inch cast-iron pan or heavy-bottom skillet over medium-high heat until it reaches 350 to 365°F.

Remove the catfish from the buttermilk soak 1 or 2 pieces at a time, allowing the excess buttermilk to drip off. Transfer the catfish pieces to the bag of seasoned cornmeal and flour, seal, and toss to coat well. Transfer to a plate and repeat with the remaining fish pieces.

Carefully lower the catfish pieces into the hot oil, working in batches so as not to crowd the pan. Fry for 4 to 8 minutes, flipping halfway through, until golden brown on the outside and cooked through in the middle. The cooking time will depend on the thickness of the fillets. Be sure to watch the heat and adjust the temperature so the fish does not burn. Transfer each batch of fried catfish to a wire rack atop a baking sheet and place in a warm oven (225°F) while frying the remaining catfish pieces. When the batches are done, squeeze lemon juice on the fillets and serve with your favorite side. In the Lowcountry, we serve our fried "fush" with a few slices of white bread and red rice!

Tuna Melt

Serves 2

- 1 small red or sweet onion, finely chopped
- 1 stalk celery, finely chopped
- ½ cup mayonnaise (preferably Duke's)
- 1 tablespoon Dijon mustard
- 2 teaspoons dried dill
- 2 teaspoons seafood seasoning
- 1 tablespoon freshly squeezed lemon juice
- 1 tablespoon sweet relish
- 1 large hard-boiled egg, chopped
- 1 5-ounce can solid white tuna in water, drained
- Freshly ground black pepper
- Kosher salt
- 2 tablespoons unsalted butter, room temperature
- 4 slices bread of your choice
- 4 slices American cheese or sharp white cheddar

In a large bowl, combine the onion, celery, mayonnaise, Dijon mustard, dill, seafood seasoning, lemon juice, relish, and egg. In the same bowl, add the tuna, breaking it up with a fork. Season generously with pepper. Taste for salt and adjust to your liking. Set aside.

Heat a large cast-iron skillet over medium heat. Add the butter to the skillet. Assemble the sandwiches with the bread, cheese, and tuna spread. Working in batches if needed, place the sandwiches in the skillet, cheese side closest to the heat, and cook, turning once and pressing down with a fish spatula to ensure good contact with the skillet, until the bread is golden brown and crisp and the cheese is melted, about 4 minutes per side. (If using cheddar, cover the pan after turning the sandwiches to ensure that the cheese melts.) Serve with your favorite side, such as chips or a salad.

Shrimp Pasta Salad

Serves 6 to 8

1 pound medium frozen shrimp, thawed

¼ cup neutral oil

Juice from ½ lemon

Kosher salt

Freshly ground black pepper

1 cup mayonnaise

¼ cup sweet relish

2 tablespoons red wine vinegar

2 teaspoons seafood seasoning

2 teaspoons garlic powder

2 teaspoons Dijon mustard

1 pound elbow macaroni, cooked according to package directions

1 stalk celery, diced

1 sweet onion, diced

½ green bell pepper, diced

¼ cup finely chopped fresh parsley

A pinch of paprika, for sprinkling

In a medium bowl, toss together the shrimp, oil, lemon juice, a pinch of salt, and pepper. Place the seasoned shrimp in a 10-inch skillet (or in a grill basket on the grill) and cook over medium-high heat, flipping once halfway through, until just cooked, about 5 minutes. Set aside.

Stir together the mayonnaise, relish, vinegar, seafood seasoning, garlic powder, and Dijon mustard in a large serving bowl. Add the cooked pasta, celery, onion, and bell pepper and toss to combine and coat with the dressing. Season to taste with salt and pepper. Add the cooked shrimp to the bowl with the pasta and toss together. Cover and refrigerate for at least 1 hour or overnight. Top the salad with the parsley and paprika right before serving.

Lowcountry Shrimp Medley

Serves 8 to 12

- 2 pounds cooked, peeled, and deveined medium shrimp
- 2 cucumbers, finely chopped (about 1½ cups)
- 1¾ cups fresh lime juice
- 3 tablespoons vegetable oil
- 1 tablespoon seafood seasoning
- 3 plum tomatoes, diced
- 1 stalk celery, finely chopped
- 2 green onions, chopped
- 1 small red onion, finely chopped
- 1 small red bell pepper, finely chopped
- 1 small green bell pepper, finely chopped
- A pinch of kosher salt
- Tortilla chips, for serving

Cut the shrimp in half and place in a medium bowl. Add the cucumbers, lime juice, vegetable oil, seafood seasoning, tomatoes, celery, green onions, red onion, red and green bell peppers, and salt. Stir well. Cover and refrigerate to marinate and chill, 30 minutes to 1 hour. Serve with chips for dipping.

Chef's note: You can make this a fun and easy party appetizer. Serve in glasses with a few chips on top. Your guests will love it!

Honey Mustard Salmon Bites

Serves 4

- 2 pounds salmon, cut into 1-inch cubes
- 2 tablespoons soy sauce
- 1 tablespoon neutral oil
- ⅓ cup honey
- ⅓ cup yellow or whole grain mustard
- 1 tablespoon lemon juice
- Kosher salt
- Freshly ground black pepper
- Green onions, sliced, and sesame seeds, for garnish (optional)
- Hot steamed white rice, for serving

Place the cubed salmon into a shallow bowl or glass container. In a small bowl or glass measuring cup, mix together the soy sauce, oil, honey, mustard, lemon juice, and a pinch of salt and pepper. Pour the marinade over the salmon and toss to coat well. For best results, allow to marinate for 30 minutes or up to 6 hours in the fridge. Heat a large skillet over medium-high heat and sear the salmon for 2 to 3 minutes, or until nice and brown, reserving any extra marinade. Flip the salmon using tongs and sear on the other side for 2 to 3 minutes, or until browned and fully cooked. Pour the remaining marinade into the skillet and cook until it comes to a slight boil and creates a sauce. Toss the salmon in the sauce to coat.

Garnish with the green onions and sesame seeds, if desired, and serve with the steamed rice.

Fish Chowder

Serves 8 as an appetizer or 4 to 6 as a main dish

- 8 slices thick-cut applewood-smoked bacon, diced
- 3 stalks celery, sliced
- 1 large yellow onion, diced
- 3 cloves garlic, minced
- 4 tablespoons (½ stick) unsalted butter
- ¼ cup all-purpose flour
- 4 cups seafood or vegetable stock
- 2 cups heavy cream
- 2 cups fresh or frozen corn kernels
- 1 pound russet potatoes, peeled and cut into large chunks
- 2 teaspoons smoked paprika
- Kosher salt
- Freshly ground black pepper
- 2 pounds tilapia or any other white fish, cut into bite-size pieces
- Fresh dill and chives, chopped, for garnish
- 8 slices thick-cut applewood-smoked bacon, cooked and crumbled, for garnish (optional)

Place a large Dutch oven over medium heat. Add the bacon and cook until the fat begins to render but the bacon is still soft, about 5 minutes. Add the celery and onion and cook until the bacon is crisp and the vegetables are tender, about 5 minutes. Stir in the garlic.

Add the butter and flour and stir until combined. Cook until the flour is bubbly, about 2 minutes. Slowly add the stock and whisk until combined. Whisk in the heavy cream.

Add the corn, potatoes, and paprika. Season with salt and pepper. Cover and cook over medium heat, stirring occasionally, until the potatoes are tender, about 15 minutes.

Add the fish to the Dutch oven. Reduce the heat to low, cover, and simmer until the fish flakes with a fork, 5 to 7 more minutes. Taste and add more salt and pepper if necessary. Spoon into serving bowls and garnish with the dill and chives. Sprinkle with the crumbled bacon, if desired.

Easy Shrimp Scampi Pasta

Serves 4

1 pound uncooked large shrimp, peeled and deveined

Kosher salt

Freshly ground black pepper

8 tablespoons (1 stick) unsalted butter, divided

6 cloves garlic, minced

½ teaspoon red pepper flakes

¼ cup dry white wine (or chicken stock)

Juice of ½ lemon (about 1 tablespoon)

1 tablespoon chopped fresh parsley

16 ounces spaghetti, cooked according to package instructions and drained

Season the shrimp with salt and pepper. Melt 4 tablespoons of the butter in a large skillet over medium heat. Add the shrimp to the skillet and cook for 1 minute per side. Stir in the garlic and red pepper flakes and cook for about 30 seconds more. Pour in the wine and let it bubble for 2 minutes. Add in the remaining 4 tablespoons of butter and the lemon juice and parsley. Once the butter melts, give it a stir and take the skillet off the heat. Add the cooked pasta to the skillet, along with a pinch of salt and pepper to taste; toss and serve.

Chef's note: If using frozen shrimp, place them in a colander under cool running water until thawed.

Sea Island Mussels

Serves 2

2 tablespoons unsalted butter, divided

1 small yellow onion, sliced

2 cloves garlic, minced

1 14.5-ounce can diced tomatoes

⅛ teaspoon cayenne pepper

½ teaspoon kosher salt

½ cup dry white wine (or chicken broth)

1 pound mussels

2 tablespoons chopped fresh parsley

2 lemon wedges

Charred bread, for serving (optional)

Melt 1 tablespoon of the butter in a large pot over medium-high heat. Add the onion and garlic and cook, stirring occasionally, until the onion begins to soften and becomes translucent, about 4 minutes. Add the tomatoes, cayenne pepper, and salt and cook for 2 minutes. Add the wine and bring to a simmer. Add the mussels, cover the pot, and cook until they open, 3 to 5 minutes. Check halfway through and transfer any open mussels to a serving bowl. Add the remaining 1 tablespoon of butter to the pot, swirl the pot a few times to incorporate the butter into the broth, and then toss the mussels with the broth. Transfer the mussels to the serving bowl, discarding any that did not open. Pour the broth over the mussels, sprinkle with the parsley and squeeze the lemon over the top. Serve with the charred bread, if desired.

Chef's note: Heat a cast-iron grill pan over medium-high heat. Add a drizzle of olive oil to a pan and grill your bread until toasted and grill marks appear, about 2 minutes per side.

Salmon *and* Potato Gratin

Serves 6

- 1 tablespoon unsalted butter
- 3 large russet potatoes, peeled and thinly sliced
- ½ teaspoon kosher salt, plus more for sprinkling
- ½ teaspoon freshly ground black pepper, plus more for sprinkling
- 1½ cups cooked salmon, broken into pieces (you can also use smoked salmon)
- 2 cups Parmesan cheese, divided (you can also use Gruyère or fontina)
- 2 cups frozen spinach, thawed and drained
- 1½ cups heavy cream
- ½ cup whole milk
- ½ cup sour cream
- ¼ cup panko breadcrumbs

Preheat the oven to 375°F.

Grease a 12-inch cast-iron skillet with the butter. Arrange half of the potatoes in the skillet. Sprinkle with salt and pepper, then layer half of the salmon pieces, ½ cup of the Parmesan cheese, and half of the spinach on top of the potatoes. Repeat this step once more, layering the potatoes, salmon, cheese, and spinach. Heat the cream, milk, ½ teaspoon salt, and ½ teaspoon pepper in a medium saucepan over medium heat until bubbles form around the edges, about 3 minutes. Remove from the heat and stir in the sour cream. Pour the cream mixture over the potatoes, salmon, and spinach in the skillet. Sprinkle with the remaining 1 cup of Parmesan cheese and the breadcrumbs. Cover tightly with aluminum foil. Bake until the potatoes can be easily pierced with a knife, about 45 minutes. Uncover and bake until the cheese and panko has browned and the edges are bubbly, about 15 more minutes. Broil for 2 minutes, if desired. Remove the skillet from the oven and serve.

Pecan-Crusted Flounder

Serves 4

- ¾ cup panko breadcrumbs
- ¾ cup pecans
- 2 teaspoons chopped fresh rosemary
- 2 teaspoons seafood seasoning, divided
- 2 large eggs
- 1¼ pounds skinless flounder fillets, pin bones removed
- ¼ cup Dijon mustard
- Nonstick cooking spray
- ½ lemon
- 8 lemon wedges, for garnish
- 4 sprigs rosemary, for garnish (optional)

Place a rimmed baking sheet in the oven and preheat the oven to 425°F.

Pulse the breadcrumbs and pecans in a food processor until finely chopped. Stir together the breadcrumb mixture, rosemary, and ½ teaspoon of the seafood seasoning in a shallow dish or plate. Whisk the eggs in a separate shallow dish until lightly beaten.

Rub the flounder fillets with the Dijon mustard and sprinkle with the remaining 1½ teaspoons of seafood seasoning. Dip the fish in the eggs, then coat with the breadcrumb mixture.

Remove the baking sheet from the oven and coat with the cooking spray. Place the fish fillets on the hot pan and spray the tops with the cooking spray. Bake until the fish flakes with a fork, 8 to 10 minutes. Remove the fish from the oven and squeeze lemon juice over the fish before serving. Garnish with the lemon wedges and rosemary sprigs, if using.

Classic Fish *and* Chips

Serves 4

- 4 large potatoes, peeled and cut into wedges
- 1 cup all-purpose flour
- 1 teaspoon baking powder
- 2 teaspoons kosher salt, divided, plus more for sprinkling
- 2 teaspoons Miss Brown's House Seasoning (page 31)
- 1 cup milk
- 1 large egg
- 1 quart vegetable oil, for frying
- 1½ pounds cod fillets
- Malt vinegar

Place the potatoes in a medium bowl and cover with cold water.

Mix the flour, baking powder, 1 teaspoon of salt, and House Seasoning together in a medium bowl.

In a separate large bowl, place the milk and egg; add the flour mixture and stir until the batter is smooth. Let stand for at least 10 minutes.

Meanwhile, heat the oil in a large pot until it reaches 350°F.

Drain the potatoes and pat them dry with a paper towel. Sprinkle the potatoes with 1 teaspoon of salt and fry them in hot oil until tender, 4 to 5 minutes; drain the potatoes on paper towels and allow them to rest for 5 minutes. Increase the oil temperature to 375°F and fry the potatoes again until golden brown and crispy. Place the fries on a wire rack atop a sheet pan. You can keep them warm and crispy in the oven at 225°F while you fry the fish. Turn the heat under the oil down to medium-high. Dredge the cod fillets in batter, one piece at a time, and place them in the hot oil. Fry the fish in batches until golden brown on all sides, or until the internal temperature reaches 145°F, about 10 minutes. Drain the cooked fish on paper towels and serve with the fries and a sprinkle of the malt vinegar.

FIVE

rice and grains

IN MY WORLD, SIDES ARE far more than an afterthought. They often get top billing. In this section, you will find recipes to accompany your main dishes. Seasonal local grains such as benne seed and millet are Lowcountry staples. But cousins, act like you know: Culturally speaking, rice is central to Gullah Geechee life—that means even if it comes along for the ride, rice is gonna show out bursting with flavor.

When our West African ancestors were taken to the Lowcountry, they brought with them their unparalleled rice-growing skills—and rice is one of the most challenging crops there is. For centuries throughout the culture, rice was part of daily meals. And cousins, when I was growing up, my mom made rice sing. So I get it from my mama! We're talking Ghanaian Jollof Rice (page 151), Fragrant Yellow Rice (page 161)—all kinds of goodies.

And where are all my vegetarians? This section will give you life. Many of the recipes here—such as my Black Bean and Rice Burgers (page 152), Gullah Spiced Rice (page 164), and Quick Island Rice and Peas (page 158)—are not only delicious but also rich in protein. Enjoy!

House Fried Rice

Serves 8

2 tablespoons neutral oil

1 yellow onion, diced

1 cup frozen stir-fry vegetable mix, thawed

2 large eggs, lightly beaten

3 cups cooked day-old rice

2 to 3 tablespoons soy sauce

2 tablespoons green onion, chopped (optional)

Heat a large skillet or wok over medium heat. Add the oil, onion, and stir-fry vegetables. Cook until tender, 4 to 5 minutes. Move the veggies to one side of the skillet, pour the beaten eggs on the other side, and scramble, 2 to 3 minutes. Once cooked, mix the eggs with the vegetable mix. Add the rice to the skillet and pour the soy sauce on top. Stir and fry the rice and veggie mixture until thoroughly incorporated and the rice has turned golden brown, about 5 minutes. Garnish with the green onion, if using, and serve.

Red Beans and Rice

Serves 6

- ½ pound dried red kidney beans, soaked overnight
- 1 tablespoon vegetable oil
- 1 tablespoon unsalted butter
- 1 13-ounce package smoked pork, beef, or turkey sausage, halved and sliced
- 1 small yellow onion, chopped
- 1 small green bell pepper, chopped
- 1 stalk celery, chopped
- 2 cloves garlic, minced
- 1½ tablespoons concentrated chicken base, such as Better Than Bouillon
- 2 teaspoons Creole seasoning
- Kosher salt
- 1 smoked turkey wing
- 1 bay leaf
- Hot cooked rice, for serving
- 1 stalk green onions, sliced, for garnish

Drain and rinse the beans. Set aside. Heat the oil and butter in a Dutch oven over medium-high heat until the butter melts. Add the sausage and cook until browned, 8 to 10 minutes. To the same pot, add the onion, bell pepper, celery, and garlic. Stir in the bouillon, Creole seasoning, and salt to taste . Cook until the vegetables begin to soften, about 8 minutes.

Add the beans, turkey wing, and enough water to cover by 2½ inches. Add the bay leaf.

Bring to a boil. Cover, reduce the heat, and simmer until the beans are tender, 2 to 2½ hours. Remove the turkey wing and the bay leaf from the pot. Remove the skin from the wing and shred the meat. Stir in meat. Spoon the beans over the hot cooked rice and sprinkle with green onions before serving.

Creamy Chicken *and* Rice Casserole

Serves 6

For the DIY cream of chicken soup

- 2½ cups chicken broth
- 1½ cups Whole milk, divided
- ¾ cup all-purpose flour
- Kosher salt
- 4 tablespoons (½ stick) unsalted butter

For the casserole

- 4 tablespoons (½ stick) unsalted butter, divided
- 1 small onion, chopped
- 1½ pounds boneless skinless chicken breast, cut into bite-size pieces
- 2 cloves garlic, minced
- Kosher salt
- 1 cup uncooked long-grain parboiled rice
- 2 cups frozen vegetables of your choice
- 1 cup sour cream
- Freshly ground black pepper
- 1½ cups hand-shredded sharp cheddar cheese, divided
- 32 buttery crackers, crushed
- 4 tablespoons (½ stick) unsalted butter, melted

TO MAKE THE CREAM OF CHICKEN SOUP:
Combine the chicken broth and ½ cup of the milk in a large saucepan. Bring to a low boil over high heat. Meanwhile, in a small bowl, whisk the flour, a pinch of salt, and the remaining 1 cup of milk until a smooth, thick mixture forms.

Pour the flour and milk mixture into the saucepan with the broth and simmer over low heat, whisking. Add the butter to the pot. Continue to simmer and whisk until the mixture is smooth and thick, 5 to 10 minutes. Turn the burner off. The soup will thicken a bit more as it cools.

TO MAKE THE CASSEROLE:
Preheat the oven to 375°F.

Melt 2 tablespoons of the butter in a large oven-safe skillet (preferably cast-iron) over medium heat. Add the onion and cook for 2 minutes. Add the chicken and cook for 3 to 4 minutes, flipping halfway through to brown both sides. Add the garlic; cook for 1 minute while stirring constantly. Add the remaining 2 tablespoons of butter, another pinch of salt, and rice to the pan. Toast the rice. Add the frozen veggies, cream of chicken soup, and sour cream. Add a few pinches of pepper and ½ cup of the cheddar and stir.

Top the casserole with the remaining 1 cup of cheddar. Combine the crackers and melted butter and sprinkle the topping over the casserole. Bake for 20 to 25 minutes, or until the top is browned and the cheese is melted.

Ghanaian Jollof Rice

Serves 8 to 10

- ¾ cup canola oil
- 1 red onion, diced
- 3 teaspoons chicken-flavored Better Than Bouillon or 3 chicken bouillon cubes
- 1 bay leaf
- 3 cloves garlic, chopped
- 1 tablespoon fresh ginger or ½ teaspoon ground ginger
- 1 Scotch bonnet or habanero pepper, seeded and chopped (optional)
- 1 cup tomato paste
- 1 large beefsteak tomato, chopped
- 3 cups water, divided
- 2 cups parboiled rice (jasmine or basmati rice will work as well), rinsed
- A few thinly slices red onions for garnish (optional)

Preheat the oven to 350°F.

In a Dutch oven over medium-high heat, add the canola oil and onion and let it cook for about 5 minutes. Add the bouillon, bay leaf, garlic, ginger, pepper (if using), tomato paste, tomato, and 2 cups of water. Stir for a few minutes to allow everything to come together and let it simmer for 15 to 20 minutes. Turn the heat off, remove the bay leaf, and use an immersion blender or standard blender to make a smooth sauce. If using a standard blender, remember that this is hot liquid, so you'll need to vent the top. Once the sauce is smooth, return it to the Dutch oven.

Add the rinsed rice. Turn the burner back on to medium-high heat, stir, and cook for 3 to 4 minutes, then add the remaining 1 cup of water on top of the rice mixture (do not mix). Put the lid on and transfer the pot onto the middle rack of the oven. Bake undisturbed for 45 minutes. Remove the pot from the oven, fluff the rice, and then put the lid back on until ready to serve. Serve with thinly sliced onion top for a pop of color, if desired.

Chef's note: Rinse the rice under cold water until the water is clear. Removing the starch ensures fluffier rice.

Black Bean *and* Rice Burgers

Serves 4

For the house sauce

½ cup mayonnaise (you can also use vegan mayo)
¼ cup ketchup
A few dashes of hot sauce
1 teaspoon dill pickle juice
Pinch of garlic powder
Pinch of paprika
Kosher salt
Freshly ground black pepper

For the burgers

2 14-ounce cans black beans, drained and rinsed
1 tablespoon Miss Brown's House Seasoning (page 31)
½ cup cooked brown rice
½ cup panko breadcrumbs
1 small yellow onion, finely diced
1 small green bell pepper, finely diced
2 cloves garlic
2 tablespoons Worcestershire sauce
2 tablespoons neutral oil
4 slices cheddar cheese or other cheese (optional)
4 buns

Optional toppings

Lettuce
Tomato
Onions
Pickles

TO MAKE THE HOUSE SAUCE:

In a small bowl, mix together the mayonnaise, ketchup, hot sauce, pickle juice, garlic powder, paprika, and salt and pepper to taste. Set aside.

TO MAKE THE BURGERS:

Add the black beans and House Seasoning to a food processor and pulse until coarsely chopped. Add the rice, breadcrumbs, onion, bell pepper, garlic, and Worcestershire sauce and pulse just until the mixture starts to come together. Transfer the mixture to a medium bowl and stir until thoroughly combined. Using wet hands, form four patties and place on a plate.

Heat a large cast-iron pan over medium-high heat and add the oil. Add the patties and cook for about 4 minutes. Flip the patties and top with the cheese, if you like. Cook until the patties are hot and the cheese has melted, 2 to 3 minutes more.

To assemble, spread each bottom bun with a thin layer of the special house sauce, then add the patty, followed with toppings and cheese of your choice, a little more sauce, and the top bun.

Easy Rice Pilaf

Serves 6

- 2 tablespoons olive oil, divided
- 3 cloves garlic, minced
- ½ large white or yellow onion, diced
- 1½ cups long-grain white rice, rinsed
- ¼ teaspoon garlic powder
- ¼ teaspoon onion powder
- ¼ teaspoon paprika
- ¼ teaspoon salt
- 3 cups chicken stock, warm
- ½ cup fresh parsley, chopped, or 1 teaspoon dried parsley

In a large skillet with a properly fitting lid, heat 1 tablespoon of the oil over medium heat. Add the garlic and onion and sauté for about 1 minute. Add the rice. Toast for 3 minutes, stirring often. Add the remaining 1 tablespoon of oil, the garlic powder, onion powder, paprika, and salt and stir to combine. Slowly add the warm stock to the pan. Turn up the heat and bring the rice mixture to a boil, then turn down the heat to medium-low (a gentle simmer), cover, and let cook for 15 minutes undisturbed (or follow the cooking time on the rice package).

After 15 minutes, remove the rice from the heat and let rest, covered, for 2 minutes.

Remove the lid, fluff with a fork, garnish with the parsley, and serve immediately.

No-Fuss Risotto

Serves 4

6 cups chicken broth

8 tablespoons (1 stick) unsalted butter

¼ cup olive oil, plus more as needed

1 large yellow onion, finely diced (about 1 cup)

5 cloves garlic, minced

2 cups arborio rice

½ cup dry white wine

Kosher salt

Freshly ground multicolor pepper

½ cup grated Parmesan cheese

Heat the chicken broth in a medium saucepan, then cover and keep warm on low heat.

Melt the butter in a large saucepan over medium heat and add the olive oil. Add the onion and sauté, stirring occasionally, until tender and translucent, 8 to 10 minutes. Add a little more oil, if necessary, then add the garlic and rice. Toast the rice for 2 to 3 minutes, then immediately add the white wine. Cook, stirring often, until the liquid is absorbed, about 2 minutes.

Add 1 cup of the broth to the pan and simmer over medium-low heat, stirring often, until the liquid is absorbed, 3 to 4 minutes. Continue to cook, adding broth by the cupful and stirring often, until the rice is tender and creamy, 28 to 32 minutes. Add salt and pepper to taste. Top with the Parmesan before serving.

Chef's note: You can add any vegetable you like to spruce it up a bit.

Geechee Ham, Egg, *and* Rice

Serves 4

- 2 tablespoons neutral oil
- 1 tablespoon unsalted butter
- 1 large yellow onion, diced
- 2 cups ham, cubed
- 4 cups medium-grain white rice, cooked and chilled
- 4 large eggs, cooked scrambled
- 2 pinches of Miss Brown's House Seasoning (page 31)

In a large skillet, heat the oil and butter over medium-high heat. Add in the onion and cubed ham and sauté for 3 to 5 minutes, or until the ham browns and the onion begins to soften. Add the rice and sauté for another 5 minutes, or until the rice begins to brown. Stir in the scrambled eggs and heat for another 2 minutes, or until the eggs and rice are heated through. Add the House Seasoning and stir. Serve hot.

Quick Island Rice *and* Peas

Serves 4 to 6

- 2 cups long-grain white rice, rinsed
- 1 13.5-ounce can unsweetened coconut milk
- 1 15.5-ounce can dark red kidney beans (do not drain)
- 1 cup water
- Heavy pinch of kosher salt
- Pinch of ground allspice
- Pinch of freshly ground black pepper
- 3 green onions
- 2 sprigs of fresh thyme or 1 teaspoon dried thyme
- 1 Scotch bonnet pepper (optional)

In a large pot, combine the rice, coconut milk, kidney beans, water, salt, allspice, and black pepper. Add the whole green onions, thyme sprigs, and whole Scotch bonnet pepper, if using, on top. Bring to a boil, then reduce the heat to low and cover with a lid. Allow to cook, covered, for 15 minutes over low heat, then remove from the heat. Leave the lid on for an additional 5 minutes.

Open the lid and remove the green onions, thyme sprigs, and Scotch bonnet pepper. Fluff the rice and beans with a fork. Serve and enjoy.

Fragrant Yellow Rice

Serves 4

- 3 tablespoons unsalted butter
- 1 cup long-grain white rice
- 2 cloves garlic, minced, or ¼ teaspoon garlic powder
- 1 teaspoon onion powder
- 1 teaspoon turmeric
- 2 cups chicken broth
- Kosher salt
- Freshly ground black pepper

Melt the butter in a large saucepan over medium heat. Add the rice and toast for 2 to 3 minutes. Add the garlic, onion powder, and turmeric and stir until well mixed in. Slowly stir in the chicken broth and raise the heat to medium-high. Add salt and pepper to taste. Bring the rice mixture to a boil, then turn the heat to low and cover the pan with a lid. Simmer for 20 minutes. Remove from the heat and fluff with a fork.

Miss Brown's Chicken *and* Wild Rice Soup

Serves 6

3 boneless, skinless chicken breasts

1 tablespoon olive oil

Kosher salt

Freshly ground black pepper

2 tablespoons unsalted butter, plus more as needed

1 yellow onion, finely diced

2 stalks celery, finely diced

1 green bell pepper, finely diced

4 cloves garlic, minced

¼ cup fresh parsley, roughly chopped, plus more for optional garnish

1 teaspoon dried thyme

1 teaspoon rubbed sage

6 cups chicken broth

2 cups wild rice, cooked according to package instructions

1 10-ounce package of frozen peas and carrots

Crusty bread, for serving (optional)

Preheat the oven to 400°F. Rub the chicken breasts with the olive oil and sprinkle both sides with salt and pepper. Place the chicken on a broiler pan or sheet pan and bake for 20 to 25 minutes. When an instant-read thermometer inserted into the center of a breast reads at least 165°F, remove the chicken from the oven. Let cool. Cut the chicken into small cubes and set aside, saving any juices.

In a Dutch oven or large pot, melt the butter over medium-high heat. Add the onion, celery, and bell pepper. Cook and stir for 3 to 4 minutes, until the onion begins to turn golden and translucent. Add the garlic, parsley, thyme, and sage. Stir and add more butter if necessary. Add the broth, any leftover chicken juice, the diced chicken, and the rice. Stir and bring to a boil over medium-high heat. Reduce the heat to medium-low, then taste. Add salt and pepper to your liking. Cover and simmer for 15 minutes. Remove the lid, add frozen peas and carrots and stir. Cover and cook for an additional 15 minutes. I like to add a little more fresh parsley on top for a pop of color. Serve warm with crusty bread, if desired.

Gullah Spiced Rice

Serves 6 to 8

- 2 tablespoons vegetable oil
- 2 cups long-grain parboiled rice
- 1 teaspoon ground cumin
- 1 teaspoon garlic powder
- 1 teaspoon sweet paprika
- ½ teaspoon celery seeds
- ½ teaspoon ground mace or nutmeg
- 1 teaspoon freshly ground black pepper
- 4 cups low-sodium chicken broth
- 1 cup tomato sauce
- 1 cup frozen corn
- ½ teaspoon kosher salt

Heat the oil in a large skillet over medium heat. Add the rice and toast, stirring constantly, until it begins to smell nutty, about 2 minutes. Stir in the cumin, garlic powder, paprika, celery seeds, mace, and pepper. Cook, stirring occasionally, 2 minutes more. Stir in the broth, tomato sauce, corn, and salt. Cover the skillet and simmer until the rice is cooked and has absorbed all the liquid, 30 to 40 minutes. Fluff with a fork before serving.

Crispy Garlic Rice

Serves 4 to 5

4 tablespoons neutral cooking oil

2 tablespoons unsalted butter

7 or 8 large cloves garlic, minced

4 cups cooked jasmine or long-grain rice (preferably a day old)

Kosher salt

In a large skillet on medium heat, place the oil, butter, and garlic. Cook the garlic until golden brown, 3 to 5 minutes. Stir occasionally. Crank the heat up to medium-high, add the rice and salt to taste. Mix the garlic and rice together until thoroughly incorporated. Turn off the heat and serve as a flavorful side dish.

SIX

good greens

OKRA, TOMATOES, CORN, COLLARDS—YOU NAME IT. There is nothing that grows we can't create a tasty meal around. And can I tell you a secret, cousins? The vegetables don't always need to be fresh. Yep, you heard me right.

I know you've heard it said that fresh is best. But there is no need to side-eye the freezer section because let's be real: It is not always practical to buy fresh produce. You need to buy the just-right amount or it will go bad. Then your hard-earned money is down the drain. Frozen vegetables are not drowning in preservatives and they are typically not overly processed. The vegetables are no less healthy. And you'll see in this section that I swap out fresh for frozen—and sometimes canned.

My point is, you don't need to let anything hold you back from enjoying good food. And I want you all to get in the kitchen and experience the joy that comes from putting together a meal for you and the people you love. Dishes like my Pan-Fried Brussels with Bacon (page 187) and Garlicky Frozen Spinach (page 184) are so fun and easy to make—in all of 10 to 15 minutes start to finish.

Vegetables and Dumplings

Serves 4 to 6

For the soup

4 tablespoons (½ stick) unsalted butter

1 large yellow onion, diced

2 stalks celery, sliced

Kosher salt

Freshly ground black pepper

2 tablespoons all-purpose flour

2 cloves garlic, chopped

6 cups vegetable stock

2 12-ounce packages frozen vegetable blend (I like the blend with broccoli and cauliflower)

1 bay leaf

For the dumplings

1 cup all-purpose flour

1 teaspoon baking powder

½ teaspoon kosher salt

2 tablespoons vegetable shortening

⅔ cup buttermilk

½ bunch of fresh parsley leaves, for serving (optional)

TO MAKE THE SOUP:

Melt the butter in a large Dutch oven over medium-high heat. Add the onion and celery and season with salt and pepper. Cook, stirring frequently with a wooden spoon and scraping up the brown bits that cling to the bottom of the pan, until the vegetables are coated in fat and slightly golden, about 3 minutes. Add the flour and stir until the vegetables are coated. Add the garlic and cook until fragrant, about 30 seconds. Add the vegetable stock, frozen vegetables, and bay leaf and bring to a boil, then lower to a simmer, cover, and cook for about 45 minutes. While the base is simmering, you can work on the dumplings.

TO MAKE THE DUMPLINGS:

Whisk together the flour, baking powder, and salt in a large bowl. Using a fork, cut the shortening into the flour mixture. Slowly add the buttermilk, gently mixing to incorporate. Now add scoops of dumpling dough over the top of the stew, about 1 tablespoon each. Cover and simmer until the dumplings double in size, about 15 minutes. Remove from the heat, discard the bay leaf, and garnish with parsley, if using.

Savory Veggie Cobbler

Serves 8

For the filling

Nonstick cooking spray

4 tablespoons (½ stick) salted butter

1 yellow onion, diced

2 stalks celery, diced

1 teaspoon kosher salt

½ teaspoon freshly ground black pepper

¼ cup all-purpose flour

1¾ cups vegetable broth

¾ cup heavy cream or whole milk

1 12-ounce package frozen mixed vegetables

For the topping

1 12-ounce box Bisquick baking mix

2 cups whole milk

1½ cups shredded yellow cheddar cheese

1 teaspoon freshly ground black pepper

1 teaspoon garlic powder

1 teaspoon onion powder

2 teaspoons Italian seasoning

4 tablespoons (½ stick) unsalted butter, melted

Preheat the oven to 375°F. Spray a 9 × 13-inch casserole dish with nonstick spray and set aside.

TO MAKE THE FILLING:
Melt the butter in a large heavy-bottom skillet over medium-high heat. Add the onion and celery and cook until tender, about 5 minutes, seasoning with the salt and pepper as the vegetables cook. This will help to sweat the onions. Sprinkle with the flour and stir until the mixture thickens. Add the broth and heavy cream and stir until the liquid thickens and turns into a gravy. Add the frozen vegetables, then simmer and stir with a wooden spoon. Taste and adjust the salt and pepper to your liking. Remove the skillet from the heat. Pour the vegetables into the prepared casserole dish.

TO MAKE THE TOPPING:
In a medium bowl, combine the Bisquick, milk, cheese, pepper, garlic powder, onion powder, and Italian seasoning. Pour the topping over the casserole, but do not mix it in! Lightly brush the melted butter on top. Bake for 55 to 60 minutes or until the topping is golden brown and the filling is bubbling.

Vegan Collards

Serves 6

- 1 tablespoon unsalted butter
- 1 tablespoon olive oil
- ½ large onion, chopped
- 2 cloves garlic, finely chopped
- 1½ cups vegetable stock, plus more if needed
- 2 teaspoons peeled, grated fresh ginger
- 2 bunches collard greens, chopped (about 1 pound)
- 2 teaspoons honey
- Kosher salt
- Freshly ground black pepper
- 2 large beefsteak tomatoes, cored and chopped

Melt the butter with the oil in a large, deep pot over medium heat. Add the onion and sauté until slightly softened, 2 to 3 minutes, then add the garlic and cook for 2 minutes more. Add the vegetable stock and ginger to the pot and bring to a simmer. Add the collard greens in batches, stirring and adding more as they wilt down. Stir in the honey and season with salt and pepper. Stir in the tomatoes, then cover and cook, adding more stock if necessary, until the greens are tender, about 20 minutes. Taste the greens and add salt and pepper if you like.

Gussied-Up Green Beans

Serves 4

2 tablespoons unsalted butter

½ medium onion, diced

2 cloves garlic, minced

2 14.25-ounce cans French-style green beans, drained

2 teaspoons distilled white vinegar

½ teaspoon onion powder

Pinch of sugar

Pinch of kosher salt

Pinch of freshly ground black pepper

Melt the butter in a 10-inch or small skillet then add the onion and garlic. Cook until the onion is slightly translucent, about 5 minutes. Add the green beans, vinegar, onion powder, sugar, salt, and pepper. Simmer, uncovered and stirring occasionally, for 3 to 4 minutes. Taste and adjust seasonings, if necessary, before serving.

Grandma's Lima Beans

Serves 8 to 10 as a side

- 1 tablespoon neutral oil
- 1 large white onion, chopped (about 1 cup)
- 3 garlic cloves, minced
- 1 pound dry lima beans, rinsed and soaked according to package directions
- 1 smoked turkey leg or wing, fully cooked (about 1 to 1½ pounds)
- 2 pinches of Miss Brown's House Seasoning (page 31)
- 2 teaspoons baking soda
- 1 bay leaf
- 5 to 6 cups water (enough to submerge the beans)
- Steamed white rice, for serving

Heat the oil in a large soup pot on medium-high heat. Add the onion and garlic. Sauté until translucent and fragrant, 4 to 5 minutes. Add the lima beans, smoked turkey, House Seasoning, baking soda, bay leaf, and water. Stir.

Cover the pot and lower the heat to medium-low. Cook for 90 minutes to 3 hours until the beans are soft. The beans are done when you can smash them against the pot very easily. Remove the bay leaf and smoked turkey leg. Using 2 forks, shred the turkey and return the meat to the pot. Taste and adjust the seasoning to your liking. Serve with white rice.

Quick Black-Eyed Peas

Serves 2

1 tablespoon unsalted butter

3 tablespoons neutral oil

½ small red onion, diced

1 medium green bell pepper, diced

1 cup diced tomatoes (fresh or canned)

4 garlic cloves, minced

1 15.5-ounce can black-eyed peas, drained and rinsed

2 teaspoons Miss Brown's House Seasoning (page 31)

Kosher salt

Freshly ground black pepper

Fresh basil or parsley, for garnish

Melt the butter with the oil in a 10-inch skillet over medium heat. Add the onion and bell pepper and sauté 2 to 3 minutes. Then add the tomatoes and garlic and cook for another 1 to 2 minutes.

Increase the heat to medium-high and add the black-eyed peas. Fry for 5 minutes, stirring occasionally to make sure all the peas are coated with the infused oil. Stir in the House Seasoning and salt and pepper to taste. Remove the peas from the heat and garnish with fresh basil or parsley.

Maple-Glazed Roasted Carrots

Serves 4

- 2 pounds carrots, washed and scrubbed, ends trimmed
- ¼ cup maple syrup
- ¼ cup packed light brown sugar
- ⅓ cup olive oil
- 2 teaspoons apple cider vinegar
- Kosher salt
- Freshly ground black pepper
- A handful of chopped fresh parsley or other fresh herbs, for garnish (optional)

Preheat the oven to 400°F and line a baking sheet with foil or parchment paper for easy cleanup. Transfer the carrots to the baking sheet and spread them out in a single layer. Set aside.

In a small bowl, whisk together the maple syrup, brown sugar, oil, and vinegar. Pour the maple mixture over the carrots. Toss and season with a pinch of salt and pepper.

Bake for 30 to 40 minutes, until tender, tossing at least once during cooking. Remove the carrots from the oven, garnish with the parsley (if desired), and serve with your entrée.

Garlicky Frozen Spinach

Serves 2 or 3

- 2 tablespoons olive oil or any neutral oil, plus more for drizzling
- 3 cloves garlic, sliced
- 1 10-ounce package frozen spinach leaves, thawed
- 2 teaspoons kosher salt
- 2 teaspoons freshly ground black pepper
- Juice of ½ lemon
- Zest of ½ lemon

Heat the olive oil in a large skillet on medium-high heat. Add the garlic and stir-fry for 20 to 30 seconds. Add the frozen spinach and sprinkle with salt and pepper. Cook, stirring, until the water evaporates, 3 to 4 minutes. Drizzle with a little more olive oil. Stir in the lemon juice and lemon zest. Serve alongside your entrée.

Cream *of* Collards

Serves 6 to 8

- 4 tablespoons (½ stick) unsalted butter
- ½ small yellow onion, diced
- 2 cloves garlic, sliced
- ¼ cup all-purpose flour
- ½ cup heavy cream
- ¼ cup whole milk
- 1 teaspoon kosher salt
- 1 teaspoon freshly ground black pepper
- 2 teaspoons red pepper flakes
- 1 bunch collard greens, cleaned, stemmed, and chopped
- Vegetable broth or water, as needed
- 1 cup shredded Parmesan cheese

Melt the butter in a large skillet or Dutch oven over medium heat. Add the onion and sauté until soft, about 5 minutes. Stir in the garlic and cook until fragrant, about 30 seconds. Add the flour to the skillet and cook until bubbly.

Slowly add the heavy cream to the skillet, whisking until combined. Add the milk, salt, pepper, and red pepper flakes. Cook until the mixture just begins to boil and thicken. Stir in the collards. Reduce the heat and simmer until the greens are tender, 5 to 7 minutes. Add a little broth or water, if needed. Stir in the Parmesan cheese and serve warm.

Pan-Fried Brussels *with* Bacon

Serves 2 to 3

6 slices bacon

½ tablespoon olive oil

1 small red onion, diced

Pinch of kosher salt

Pinch of freshly ground black pepper

1 16-ounce package frozen Brussels sprouts, thawed, halved, and patted dry

Cook the bacon in a large skillet over medium-high heat until crisp. Drain on paper towels, crumble, and set aside. Heat the olive oil in the same skillet over medium-high heat. Add the onion, salt, and pepper and cook until soft. Add the Brussels sprouts, cut side down. Cook until browned, turning once or twice, 7 to 9 minutes total. Add the bacon and stir until heated through, about 1 minute.

Crispy Oven-Roasted Broccoli

Serves 2

- 1 pound fresh broccoli florets (or frozen broccoli, thawed, drained, and patted dry)
- 6 tablespoons (¾ stick) unsalted butter, melted, divided
- 1 tablespoon Miss Brown's House Seasoning (page 31)
- ⅓ cup plain panko breadcrumbs
- Zest of 1 lemon
- Pinch of garlic powder
- Pinch of kosher salt

Place the broccoli on a large baking sheet or cast-iron skillet, drizzle with 3 tablespoons of the melted butter, and season with House Seasoning. Mix well. In a small bowl, mix together the breadcrumbs, lemon zest, garlic powder, and salt. Sprinkle the seasoned breadcrumbs over the broccoli, drizzle the remaining 3 tablespoons of butter on top, and bake at 425°F for 20 minutes.

Country Fried Corn

Serves 4

2 slices of thick-sliced bacon, cut into chunks

2 tablespoons unsalted butter, plus more if needed

1 Vidalia onion, diced

1 medium green bell pepper, diced

4 cups frozen corn kernels, thawed

2 cloves garlic, minced

Kosher salt

Freshly ground black pepper

2 cups grape tomatoes, halved

Heat a large cast-iron or nonstick skillet over medium heat. Add the bacon and cook until crispy, about 3 minutes. Remove the bacon from the skillet with a slotted spoon and place on paper towels, reserving the drippings in the skillet.

Increase the heat to medium-high. Add the butter and heat until melted. Add the onion and bell pepper and cook until the vegetables are softened and begin to brown, 4 to 5 minutes. Stir in the corn and garlic and season with salt and pepper. Add the tomatoes and cook until the corn is softened and the tomatoes begin to release their liquid, about 5 minutes more. Stir in the bacon and serve.

Josephine's Sweet Peas

Serves 4 to 6

- 2 smoked turkey or ham neck bones (or any smoked meat)
- ½ medium Vidalia or sweet yellow onion, chopped
- 4 cups water
- 2 15-ounce cans sweet peas, drained
- Heavy pinch of garlic powder
- Heavy pinch of onion powder
- Pinch of kosher salt
- Pinch of freshly ground black pepper
- 2 pinches of sugar

In a large pot over medium-high heat, boil the neck bones and onion uncovered in the water until the water has reduced to nearly half. Add the peas to the pot. Season with the garlic powder, onion powder, salt, black pepper, and sugar. Stir, taste, and adjust the seasoning to your liking. Reduce the heat to simmer, cover, and cook for 20 minutes. Remove the pot from the heat. Take the neck bones out and shred as much of the meat as you can. Return the meat to the pot, mix, and serve.

Four Bean Salad

Serves 6

Kosher salt
2 pounds fresh green beans, trimmed
⅓ cup olive oil
2 tablespoons honey
2 tablespoons yellow mustard
2 tablespoons apple cider vinegar
2 cloves garlic, grated or minced
Freshly ground black pepper
2 cups cooked baby lima beans, canned or frozen
1 15-ounce can kidney beans, rinsed and drained
1 15-ounce can white beans, such as cannellini or great northern beans, rinsed and drained
½ cup sliced almonds
¼ cup dried cranberries
4 scallions, thinly sliced

Bring a pot of salted water to a boil and prepare a bowl of ice water. Add the green beans to the boiling water and cook until still very crisp, 1 to 2 minutes, then transfer to the ice water until cool. Cut in half.

Whisk together the oil, honey, mustard, vinegar, and garlic in a large bowl. Season lightly with salt and pepper. Add the green beans, lima beans, kidney beans, white beans, almonds, cranberries, and scallions and toss until everything is coated. Season to taste. Serve immediately or cover and refrigerate until ready to serve, up to 1 day.

Ma's Cucumber Pasta Salad

Serves 6

Kosher salt

½ pound uncooked spaghetti

1 16-ounce bottle Italian salad dressing

2 English cucumbers, sliced

8 ounces cherry tomatoes, sliced in half

1 tablespoon garlic powder

1 tablespoon onion powder

⅓ cup green onions, diced

Freshly ground black pepper

Bring a large pot of heavily salted water to a boil. Place the spaghetti in the pot, cook for 8 to 10 minutes, until al dente, and drain. In a large bowl, toss the cooked pasta with the Italian dressing, cucumbers, tomatoes, garlic powder, onion powder, and green onions. Sprinkle with a little salt and pepper. Taste and adjust to your liking. Cover and refrigerate for at least 30 minutes (preferably overnight) before serving.

Pantry Chili

Serves 8

2 tablespoons vegetable oil

1 green bell pepper, chopped

1 yellow onion, chopped

1 pound 80/20 ground beef

2 cloves garlic, minced

1 28-ounce can crushed tomatoes

1 28-ounce can diced tomatoes, undrained

1 15.5-ounce can black beans, rinsed and drained

1 15.5-ounce can dark kidney beans, rinsed and drained

1 15.5-ounce can light kidney beans, rinsed and drained

2½ cups beef broth

3 tablespoons chili powder

Pinch of ground cinnamon

Kosher salt

Freshly ground black pepper

For serving

Sour cream

Green onion, chopped

Shredded sharp cheddar cheese

In a large Dutch oven or sauce pot, heat the oil over medium-high heat. Add the bell pepper and onion and cook 2 to 3 minutes, then add the ground beef. Cook until beef is browned, 8 to 10 minutes. Add the garlic, crushed tomatoes, diced tomatoes, black beans, dark kidney beans, and light kidney beans. Add the beef broth, then stir in the chili powder and cinnamon. Bring the chili to a boil. Cover, reduce the heat to low, and cook 1 hour. Season with salt and pepper.

To serve, divide the chili between eight serving bowls. Top with the sour cream, green onions, and cheese.

SEVEN

flour, sugar, and butter

AT ANY GIVEN TIME, MOST KITCHENS have the foundational elements for a scrumptious dessert. When I say you don't need to overthink the sweet-touch finisher to a great meal, please believe me.

From ingredients as simple as flour, eggs, butter, and sugar, you can make something mouthwateringly delicious. It all depends on just how decadent you want to go. When you want to keep it simple, you can't go wrong with my Almond Sour Cream Pound Cake (page 236). When you're going for something rich and indulgent, I've got you covered there as well. The Warm Sticky Apple Pudding (page 238) is phenomenal, and nothing says "easy like Sunday morning" like my Peach Pudding (page 233).

Ma's Goodie Bars

Serves 16

- Nonstick cooking spray
- 2 cups crushed graham crackers (about 12 sheets)
- 8 tablespoons (1 stick) unsalted butter, melted
- 1 teaspoon kosher salt
- 2 cups dark or semisweet chocolate chips
- 1 cup chopped pecans
- 1 cup shredded sweetened coconut flakes
- 1 14-ounce can sweetened condensed milk

Preheat the oven to 350°F. Coat a 9 × 13-inch baking pan with cooking spray and set aside.

Stir the graham cracker crumbs, melted butter, and salt in a medium bowl until thoroughly combined. Press the crust mixture into the bottom of the prepared pan in an even layer.

Sprinkle the chocolate chips, pecans, and coconut over the crust. Pour the condensed milk evenly over the top and spread with a spatula to level it out.

Bake until the edges are golden brown and the middle is set, 30 to 40 minutes. Let cool completely before slicing into 16 bars.

Chocolate Peanut Butter Saltines

Serves 16

28 to 35 saltine crackers
1 cup (2 sticks) unsalted butter
1 cup packed light brown sugar
1 cup peanut butter
Pinch of kosher salt
1 teaspoon vanilla extract
2 cups semisweet chocolate chips, divided
¼ cup chopped salted peanuts

Preheat the oven to 375°F.

Line a baking sheet with parchment paper, then add the saltine crackers in a single layer, using enough crackers to cover the baking sheet.

In a saucepan over medium-high heat, melt the butter, then add the brown sugar. Stir and cook until the mixture comes to a slight boil. Turn the heat down to medium-low, but keep your eye on the pot. Add the peanut butter and salt to the saucepan. Continue to cook on medium-low heat, stirring frequently, until everything melts together, about 3 minutes. Remove the pot from the heat and stir in the vanilla extract.

Pour the peanut butter–caramel mixture over the saltine crackers, spreading with a spatula to evenly coat the crackers. Bake for 7 minutes, until the caramel is hot and bubbly throughout. Sprinkle the chocolate chips over the top and bake for 5 minutes more, until the chocolate melts.

Turn the oven off and remove the tray from the oven and use a spoon or spatula to swirl the chocolate into an even layer. Top with the chopped peanuts and place in the refrigerator to set. Break the peanut butter saltine bark into large pieces and enjoy!

Chef's note: For less mess, spray a measuring cup with nonstick cooking spray when measuring out the peanut butter.

Chocolate Chip Cookies

Makes 1 dozen

- 3 cups all-purpose flour
- 1 teaspoon baking soda
- ¼ teaspoon kosher salt
- 1 cup (2 sticks) butter, room temperature
- ½ cup granulated sugar
- 1¼ cups packed dark brown sugar
- 2 large eggs, lightly beaten
- 1 teaspoon vanilla extract
- 2½ cups semisweet or dark chocolate chips, divided

Line two baking sheets with parchment paper.

Whisk together the flour, baking soda, and salt in a medium bowl.

Use a stand mixer or an electric hand mixer to lightly beat the butter, granulated sugar, and brown sugar for about 30 seconds. Add in the eggs one at a time, beating briefly after each egg. Now add the vanilla extract. Add the dry ingredients a little at a time and beat to combine. Set aside about ¼ cup of the chocolate chips for the topping, then mix in the remainder.

Form balls of dough with a large ice cream scoop. Press a few of the reserved chocolate chips right on top of each ball. This will help to create little pools of chocolate. Place 6 balls of dough on each prepared baking sheet and place them in the freezer for at least an hour and up to overnight.

When ready to bake, preheat the oven to 375°F. Bake one sheet of cookies at a time, until the edges and spots on top are golden but the insides are still slightly doughy, 15 to 18 minutes.

Cornflake Clusters

Makes about 30 clusters

6 cups plain cornflakes cereal
1 cup light corn syrup
½ cup granulated sugar
½ cup packed light brown sugar
1 teaspoon kosher salt
1 cup creamy peanut butter
1 teaspoon vanilla extract
Sprinkles (optional)

Line a baking sheet with parchment paper. Put the cornflakes in a large bowl and set aside.

In a medium saucepan, combine the corn syrup, granulated sugar, brown sugar, and salt. Cook over medium heat, stirring constantly to prevent burning, until the mixture just begins to bubble, 2 to 3 minutes. Immediately remove the saucepan from the heat and add the peanut butter and vanilla. Stir until smooth and velvety. Pour the mixture over the corn flakes and use a large rubber spatula or wooden spoon to fold the mixture together.

Once the cornflakes are well coated, use a large cookie scoop or two spoons to portion the mixture out onto the prepared baking sheet. Work quickly to prevent the mixture from firming up. Top with sprinkles, if desired, to spruce it up a bit. Allow the clusters to cool completely before serving. Store in an airtight container at room temperature for up to a week.

Chef's note: You can replace the peanut butter with chocolate chips and/or toffee chips.

Grandma Josephine's Sweet Potato Pie

Serves 8 to 12

- 2 pounds fresh sweet potatoes, boiled with skin on until fork-tender
- ½ cup pulpless orange juice
- 1 cup (2 sticks) unsalted butter, melted
- 2 cups sugar
- 3 teaspoons vanilla extract
- ¾ cup heavy cream
- 2 teaspoons pumpkin spice
- 1 teaspoon kosher salt
- 5 large eggs, divided
- 2 deep-dish refrigerated piecrusts
- 1 tablespoon water

Preheat the oven to 350°F.

Remove the peel from the potatoes and cut them up into large chunks. Place them in a food processor with the orange juice and process until smooth. You may need to do this step in two batches, depending on the size of your processor. The end result should be a smooth sweet potato puree—no clumps or strings! In a large bowl, combine the sweet potato puree, melted butter, sugar, vanilla, heavy cream, pumpkin spice, and salt. Mix until fully incorporated.

In a small bowl, whisk 4 of the eggs and fold them into the sweet potato mixture. Set aside. Poke holes into the bottom of each piecrust. In the small bowl, whisk together the remaining egg with the water to make an egg wash. Brush the egg wash on the edges of the piecrusts.

Evenly divide the filling among the piecrusts. Bake for 50 minutes or until set. If the crusts start to brown before the center is set, loosely cover with foil. The filling will be slightly jiggly, but it is ready when a toothpick inserted into the center comes out almost clean. Let the pies cool to room temperature on a wire rack before slicing.

Sweet Cornbread Cake

Serves 4 to 6

1 cup yellow cornmeal
1 cup all-purpose flour
½ teaspoon baking soda
½ teaspoon kosher salt
1 cup (2 sticks) unsalted butter
½ cup buttermilk
½ cup milk
½ cup sugar
2 large eggs
Unsalted butter, softened, for serving
Honey, for serving

Preheat the oven to 375°F.

Combine the cornmeal, flour, baking soda, and salt in a bowl. Mix well and set aside.

Melt the butter in a 10-inch cast-iron skillet or large oven-safe pan over medium-high heat. Transfer the melted butter to a medium bowl, add the buttermilk, milk, sugar, and eggs and whisk until well blended. Pour in the cornmeal mixture and beat until very few lumps remain.

Pour the batter into the hot skillet and bake for 25 to 30 minutes, or until a toothpick inserted in the center comes out clean. Transfer the skillet to a wire cooling rack and allow the cake to cool slightly before slicing. Serve with butter and a drizzle of honey.

Berry Dump Cake

Serves 6

- Nonstick cooking spray
- 4 cups fresh or frozen mixed berries
- ¼ cup sugar
- 2 tablespoons cornstarch
- 1 tablespoon freshly squeezed lemon juice
- 1 teaspoon vanilla extract
- 1 15.25-ounce box vanilla cake mix
- 8 tablespoons (1 stick) unsalted butter, cut into cubes
- Vanilla ice cream, for serving

Preheat the oven to 350°F. Spray a 9-inch square baking dish with the nonstick cooking spray.

Combine the berries, sugar, cornstarch, lemon juice, and vanilla in a medium bowl. Toss to coat the berries. Pour the mixture into the prepared baking dish, then spread the cake mix over the top in an even layer. Scatter the butter cubes over the top. Cover the baking dish with aluminum foil and bake until the top is puffed and golden and the fruit is bubbling, about 40 minutes. Remove the foil and continue baking for 5 minutes more.

Let the cake cool slightly before scooping and serving with vanilla ice cream.

Butter Pecan Cookies

Makes 30 small cookies

- 8 tablespoons (1 stick) unsalted butter, softened, plus more for the baking sheets
- 1 cup packed light brown sugar
- 1 large egg, beaten, room temperature
- 1 teaspoon vanilla extract
- 2 cups all-purpose flour, plus more for dusting
- ½ teaspoon baking soda
- ½ teaspoon cream of tartar
- 1 teaspoon kosher salt
- ½ teaspoon ground cinnamon
- 1 cup chopped pecans

In a large bowl, cream the butter and brown sugar with a hand mixer. Add the egg and vanilla; beat well. Combine the flour, baking soda, cream of tartar, salt, and cinnamon in a separate large bowl and add to the creamed butter mixture. Fold in the pecans.

On a lightly floured surface, shape the dough into three 10 × 1-inch logs. Tightly wrap each log in waxed paper and freeze for at least 12 hours.

When ready to bake, preheat the oven to 350°F. Grease three baking sheets with unsalted butter or nonstick spray. Cut the logs into ⅜-inch slices and place on the prepared baking sheets. Bake for 6 to 8 minutes. Remove the cookies to a wire rack to cool.

Easy Key Lime Pie

Serves 8 to 10

For the crust

1½ cups crushed graham crackers (about 9 sheets)

8 tablespoons (1 stick) unsalted butter, melted

3 tablespoons sugar

¼ teaspoon kosher salt

For the filling

2 28-ounce cans sweetened condensed milk

6 large egg yolks

1 cup key lime juice

Zest of 1 small lime, plus more for optional garnish

2 teaspoons vanilla extract

Whipped cream topping (optional)

1 lime, thinly sliced into rounds, for garnish (optional)

TO MAKE THE CRUST:
Preheat the oven to 350°F.

In a medium bowl, combine the graham cracker crumbs with the butter, sugar, and salt. Mix thoroughly and press the mixture into the bottom and up the sides of a pie dish. Bake for 10 minutes. Remove from the oven and allow to cool on a wire rack. Reduce the oven temperature to 325°F.

TO MAKE THE FILLING:
In a medium bowl, whisk together the sweetened condensed milk, egg yolks, key lime juice, zest, and vanilla.

Pour the filling into the baked crust, and bake until set but still slightly jiggly in the center, 20 minutes. Cool completely, then refrigerate several hours or overnight. Before serving, top with the whipped cream, lime slices, and lime zest, if desired.

Peach Cobbler

Serves 8 to 10

- 1 cup all-purpose flour
- 1 tablespoon baking powder
- ½ teaspoon kosher salt
- 1½ cups granulated sugar, divided
- 1 cup whole milk
- 8 tablespoons (1 stick) unsalted butter, melted
- 2 16-ounce packages frozen peaches
- ½ cup packed light brown sugar
- 2 tablespoons water
- 1 tablespoon freshly squeezed lemon juice
- 1 teaspoon ground cinnamon
- 1 teaspoon ground nutmeg
- ½ teaspoon vanilla extract
- Ice cream, for serving

Preheat the oven to 375°F.

In a large bowl, whisk together the flour, baking powder, salt, and 1 cup of the granulated sugar. Stir in the milk, mixing just until combined.

Pour the melted butter into a 9 × 13-inch baking dish, tilting the dish to coat it evenly. Pour the batter over the butter in the baking dish, then set aside. Do not stir.

In a large saucepan, bring the peaches, brown sugar, water, lemon juice, cinnamon, nutmeg, and the remaining ½ cup granulated sugar to a boil. Cook for 2 minutes. Turn off the heat and stir in the vanilla. Pour the peach mixture into the baking dish without disturbing the batter layer. Bake until golden brown and puffed on top, 45 to 50 minutes. Let cool slightly before serving with your favorite ice cream.

Homemade Nutter Butter Cookies

Makes 16 cookies

For the cookies

1½ cups all-purpose flour
1 teaspoon baking soda
1 teaspoon cornstarch
8 tablespoons (1 stick) unsalted butter, room temperature
1 cup packed light brown sugar
1 cup creamy peanut butter
1 large egg
1 teaspoon vanilla extract

For the peanut butter filling

1 cup creamy peanut butter
1 cup confectioners' sugar
¼ cup heavy cream, plus more if needed
2 teaspoons vanilla extract

TO MAKE THE COOKIES:

Preheat the oven to 350°F. Line a cookie sheet with parchment paper and set aside.

In a medium bowl, whisk together the flour, baking soda, and cornstarch. Set aside.

In a separate large bowl, using a hand mixer or a stand mixer with the paddle attachment, cream together the butter and brown sugar. Mix until fluffy with no visible lumps. Add the peanut butter and mix together until smooth, scrapping down the sides as you go. Add the egg and vanilla and mix until well combined.

Add the dry ingredients to the peanut butter mixture and mix just until a moist dough forms. Make sure you scrape down the sides of the bowl. Divide the dough into 1 tablespoon portions. Roll one portion into two balls. Place the balls ¼ inch apart on the prepared cookie sheet and flatten the dough until it's about ½ inch thick. Repeat with the remaining dough. Use a fork to make a crosshatch pattern on each cookie. Bake until just starting to brown around the edges, about 12 minutes. Transfer the cookies to a wire rack and cool completely. While the cookies are cooling, make the filling.

TO MAKE THE PEANUT BUTTER FILLING:

Cream together the peanut butter, confectioners' sugar, heavy cream, and vanilla until smooth. Add more heavy cream if the mixture is too thick. Transfer the filling to a piping bag. Pipe the filling on the bottom side of one cookie at a time, then top with another cookie facing up. Repeat this process for the remaining cookies and serve.

Gooey Cake Bars

Makes 12 bars

- Nonstick cooking spray
- 1 box yellow cake mix
- 8 tablespoons (1 stick) unsalted butter, melted
- 4 large eggs, divided
- 8 ounces full-fat cream cheese, room temperature
- 1 teaspoon vanilla extract
- 3 cups confectioners' sugar

Preheat the oven to 350°F. Grease a 9 × 13-inch baking pan with nonstick spray and set aside.

In a medium bowl, stir together the cake mix, melted butter, and 1 of the eggs. Mix until smooth and well combined. Press the dough evenly over the bottom of the prepared baking pan. Set aside.

In a separate large bowl, beat the cream cheese until it's fluffy. Add the remaining 3 eggs one at a time, then add the vanilla and beat until smooth, 1 or 2 minutes. Add the confectioners' sugar and continue to beat until well combined. Pour the mixture over the crust and bake until the edges are set and the center is slightly jiggly, 25 to 30 minutes. When done, remove the cake from the oven and let it cool completely before cutting it into 12 equal bars.

Lemon Snowball Cookies

Makes 35 cookies

1 cup (2 sticks) unsalted butter, softened

1½ cups confectioners' sugar, divided

1 teaspoon vanilla extract

2 cups all-purpose flour

Juice of 1 lemon

Zest of 2 lemons, divided

Preheat the oven to 350°F. Line two baking sheets with parchment paper and set aside.

In a large bowl, cream the butter and 1 cup of the confectioners' sugar until light and airy. Add the vanilla and gradually beat in the flour. Stir in the lemon juice and half of the lemon zest. Shape each tablespoon of dough into a 1-inch ball. Place the balls about 2 inches apart on the prepared baking sheets. Bake until light brown, 12 to 15 minutes. Roll the cookies while still warm in the remaining ½ cup of confectioners' sugar. Place on wire racks. Top with the remaining lemon zest and cool.

Kitchen Sink Blondies

Makes 12 bars

- Nonstick cooking spray
- 1¾ cups all-purpose flour
- 1 teaspoon baking powder
- ½ teaspoon kosher salt
- 12 tablespoons (1½ sticks) unsalted butter, melted and slightly cooled
- 1½ cups packed light brown sugar
- 2 large eggs, room temperature
- 4 teaspoons vanilla extract
- 1½ cups semisweet chocolate chips
- 1 cup nuts (whatever you have on hand)
- 1 cup broken pretzels
- 1 cup chocolate candy (I use M&Ms)

Position a rack in the middle of the oven; preheat the oven to 350°F. Grease a 9 × 13-inch baking pan with cooking spray or line it with parchment paper, leaving some paper out on the sides to create an overhang for easy removal.

Whisk the flour, baking powder, and salt together in a medium bowl; set aside.

Whisk the melted butter and brown sugar together in a large bowl until combined. Add the eggs and vanilla and mix well.

Using a rubber spatula, fold the dry ingredients into the egg mixture until just combined; do not overmix. Fold in the chocolate chips, nuts, pretzel pieces, and candy. Turn the batter into the prepared pan, smoothing the top with the rubber spatula. Bake until the top is shiny, cracked, and light golden brown, 25 to 30 minutes. Do not overbake; you want the blondies to be slightly underdone to create a gooey center. Cool the pan on a wire rack until it reaches room temperature. Remove from the pan by lifting the parchment overhang (if using); transfer to a cutting board, cut into 12 large bars, and serve. If you sprayed the pan with nonstick cooking spray, you can cut the bars directly in the pan.

Bourbon Transparent Pie

Serves 10 to 12

8 tablespoons (1 stick) unsalted butter, melted

2½ cups sugar

1 cup heavy whipping cream

4 large eggs, beaten

2 teaspoons vanilla extract

2 tablespoons bourbon (optional)

2 tablespoons all-purpose flour

1 9-inch deep-dish pie shell

Whipped cream, for serving

Preheat the oven to 375°F.

Place the butter and sugar in the mixing bowl of a stand mixer with the paddle attachment, or you can use a large bowl and a hand mixer. Cream the butter and sugar together on medium speed until light and fluffy, 2 to 3 minutes. Add the whipping cream and mix on high speed until the cream has started to thicken up a bit and the mixture is light and fluffy, about 2 minutes. Beat in the eggs one at a time, then add the vanilla, bourbon (if using), and flour and mix well.

Pour the batter into the unbaked pie shell and cover just the edges of the crust with foil or a silicone piecrust cover. Bake for about 45 minutes, or until the top is golden brown and no longer jiggly in the center. Cool completely before serving with a dollop of whipped cream.

Peach Pudding

Serves 6

- 4 cups whole milk
- 1 cup plus 2 tablespoons sugar, divided
- ½ cup cornstarch
- 1 teaspoon vanilla extract
- ¼ teaspoon kosher salt
- 1 cup heavy cream
- 4 ounces cream cheese, room temperature
- 1 cup peach preserves
- 1 11-ounce box Nilla Wafers
- 2 pounds frozen sliced peaches, thawed

Bring 2 inches of water to a boil in a medium saucepan. In a medium heatproof glass bowl, whisk together the milk, 1 cup of the sugar, the cornstarch, vanilla, and salt and place the bowl on top of the boiling water (double boiler method). Reduce the heat to a simmer, and cook, whisking constantly, until the pudding has thickened and coats the back of a wooden spoon, about 20 minutes. Remove from the heat. Press a piece of plastic wrap onto the surface of the pudding to prevent a skin from forming. Let it cool completely.

With an electric hand mixer, whip the heavy cream, cream cheese, and the remaining 2 tablespoons of sugar. Fold the whipped cream cheese into the cooled pudding.

In a 9 × 13 glass serving dish or trifle dish, build the peach pudding: Using about a quarter of the pudding mixture, spread a thick layer on the bottom of the dish. Scatter about a quarter of the preserves on top, then use a butter knife to swirl the preserves into the pudding. Layer a third of the cookies on top of the pudding, and a third of the peach slices on top of the cookies. Repeat twice more. Top the last layer of peaches with the last of the pudding and swirl the remaining preserves into it. Refrigerate, covered, until ready to serve.

Ambrosia Salad

Serves 6 to 8

- 1 cup sour cream
- 1 8-ounce tub frozen whipped topping, thawed
- 1 15-ounce can fruit cocktail, slightly drained
- 1 11-ounce can mandarin oranges, drained
- 1½ cups mini marshmallows
- ½ cup pecans, toasted and chopped (optional)

Fold the sour cream and whipped topping together in a large bowl. Add the fruit cocktail, oranges, marshmallows, and pecans, if using. Continue to fold until everything is thoroughly mixed. Serve chilled.

Almond Sour Cream Pound Cake

Serves 6 to 8

- 1 cup (2 sticks) butter, softened, plus more for the pan
- 3 cups all-purpose flour, plus more for the pan
- 2 cups granulated sugar
- 1½ cups packed light brown sugar
- ½ teaspoon baking soda
- ¼ teaspoon kosher salt
- 6 large eggs, room temperature
- 2 teaspoons almond extract
- 1 teaspoon vanilla extract
- 1 cup sour cream
- ½ cup sliced almonds, divided
- Confectioners' sugar (optional)

Preheat the oven to 325°F. Grease and flour a nonstick 12-cup standard Bundt pan.

Add the butter, granulated sugar, and brown sugar to the bowl of a stand mixer and beat on medium speed until light and fluffy, about 2 minutes. Meanwhile, whisk together the flour, baking soda, and salt in a medium bowl. Reduce the mixer speed to low and add the eggs one at a time, allowing each to mix in completely. Once the eggs have been incorporated, add the almond and vanilla extracts and the sour cream and beat until just combined. Add the flour mixture a little at a time, then mix in ¼ cup of the almonds.

Sprinkle the remaining ¼ cup of almonds over the bottom of the prepared Bundt pan, then pour the batter on top. Bake for 55 to 60 minutes, or until a toothpick comes out clean. Remove the Bundt pan from the oven and transfer it to a wire rack to cool completely. Once the cake has cooled, invert it onto a serving plate and sprinkle generously with confectioners' sugar, if desired.

Warm Sticky Apple Pudding

Serves 6 to 8

For the cake

- 8 tablespoons (1 stick) unsalted butter, softened, plus more for the pan
- 5 Gala or Pink Lady apples, peeled and shredded
- 1 cup apple cider
- 2 cups all-purpose flour
- 1½ teaspoons baking powder
- 1½ teaspoons baking soda
- ½ teaspoon fine sea salt
- ½ cup packed light brown sugar
- ½ cup packed dark brown sugar
- 2 tablespoons molasses
- 1 teaspoon vanilla extract
- 3 large eggs, room temperature

For the sauce

- 8 tablespoons (1 stick) unsalted butter
- 2¼ cups milk
- ¼ cup apple juice
- 3 cups packed dark brown sugar
- ½ teaspoon fine sea salt
- 1 tablespoon vanilla extract
- Ice cream, for serving (optional)

TO MAKE THE CAKE:

Butter a 9 × 13-inch baking dish and set aside. Preheat the oven to 350°F.

In a heavy-bottom saucepan or skillet, place the apples and apple cider. Cook over medium heat until the apples have softened and the liquid has been absorbed, about 10 minutes. Turn the heat off and set aside.

In a medium bowl, whisk together the flour, baking powder, baking soda, and salt. Set aside.

In a large bowl with an electric hand or stand mixer, cream together the butter, light brown sugar, dark brown sugar, molasses, and vanilla until fluffy and well combined. Add the eggs one at a time, mixing the first one in before adding the next. Add the dry ingredients and stir to combine, scraping the sides as needed.

Add the cooked apples to the cake batter and mix them in fully.

Pour the batter in the prepared baking dish and smooth it out. Bake for 25 to 30 minutes, until the cake is dark golden brown and a toothpick inserted into the center comes out clean.

TO MAKE THE SAUCE:

Melt the butter in a medium saucepan over medium-low heat. Add the milk, apple juice, brown sugar, and salt. Cook, whisking continuously, for 4 minutes. Take the pan off the heat and stir in the vanilla, then set aside.

When the cake comes out of the oven, use a fork to poke holes all over it. Pour half of the sauce over the cake and let it sit for 15 minutes to absorb the sauce. Serve the cake warm with more sauce over each slice and a scoop of ice cream, if desired.

Mason Jar Vanilla Ice Cream

Serves 2

- 1 cup heavy whipping cream, cold
- 2 tablespoons sugar
- 1½ teaspoons vanilla
- Heavy pinch of coarse salt
- Mix-ins of your choice (for example, fruit, sprinkles, or crumbled cookies)

Put the whipping cream, sugar, vanilla, salt, and any mix-ins you're using in a 16-ounce wide-mouth freezer-safe mason jar. Seal tightly with the lid, and shake vigorously until the contents have about doubled in volume and have the consistency of brownie batter, 4 to 5 minutes. (It's an arm workout, but don't skip this part!)

Freeze the jar until the ice cream takes on the consistency of soft serve, 2 to 3 hours, shaking every 30 minutes or so to prevent the ice cream from becoming icy and any mix-ins from falling to the bottom.

Candied Baked Sweet Potato

Serves 4

- 4 large sweet potatoes
- 4 tablespoons (½ stick) unsalted butter
- ⅓ cup packed light brown sugar
- ¼ cup plus 1 tablespoon orange juice, no pulp
- 1 teaspoon ground cinnamon
- 1 teaspoon pure vanilla extract
- Pinch of ground cloves
- Pinch of kosher salt

Preheat the oven to 400°F.

Wash and scrub the sweet potatoes. Pat them dry and place them on a baking sheet lined with parchment paper. Completely wrap each potato in aluminum foil. With a fork, pierce each sweet potato several times to allow steam to release. Bake for 40 to 60 minutes or until soft.

While the potatoes are baking, melt the butter in a medium pot over medium-high heat. Add the brown sugar and stir until thoroughly blended. Stir in the orange juice, cinnamon, vanilla, cloves, and salt. Cook for 3 to 4 minutes until the mixture begins to turn into a syrup. Once the potatoes are done, split them lengthwise and evenly distribute the syrup over the potatoes. Enjoy as a dessert or as a sweet side dish.

Lemon Strawberry Cheesecake Bars

Serves 8 to 10

For the crust

1 11-ounce box vanilla wafer cookies

3 tablespoons granulated sugar

1 teaspoon lemon zest, plus more for garnish

¼ teaspoon kosher salt

12 tablespoons (1½ sticks) unsalted butter, melted

For the filling

1 cup heavy cream

3 8-ounce blocks full-fat cream cheese, room temperature

2 teaspoons vanilla extract

½ teaspoon lemon zest, plus more for garnish

2 teaspoons lemon juice

2 cups confectioners' sugar

1½ cups sour cream, room temperature

1 quart strawberries, sliced

TO MAKE THE CRUST:
Line a 9 × 13-inch baking dish with parchment paper, leaving a 2-inch overhang on the sides.

Seal the cookies in a plastic bag. Use a rolling pin or meat mallet to crush the cookies into fine crumbs. Pour the crumbs into a large bowl and add the granulated sugar, lemon zest, and salt. Pour the melted butter into the bowl and mix thoroughly with a rubber spatula. Firmly press the crumb mixture into the baking dish in an even layer. Freeze while you make the filling.

TO MAKE THE FILLING:
Beat the heavy cream in a medium bowl with an electric mixer until stiff peaks form. Set aside.

Beat the cream cheese, vanilla, lemon zest, and lemon juice in a large bowl until fluffy and light, 3 to 4 minutes. Add the confectioners' sugar and sour cream. Beat until just combined, making sure there are no lumps. Fold in the whipped cream. Remove the crust from the freezer. Pour the filling over the crust and spread in an even layer. Refrigerate for at least 4 hours and up to overnight.

Use the parchment overhang to lift the dessert out of the baking dish. When ready to serve, arrange the strawberries on top and sprinkle with lemon zest. Slice into bars and serve chilled.

This cookbook is a tribute to the simple, nourishing meals that brought my family together around the table—day after day, year after year.

I want to express my deepest gratitude to my family, whose resourcefulness, creativity, and love for "Making Do" laid the foundation for this collection. Their ability to turn humble ingredients into comforting, delicious meals has always inspired me.

To my mom and grandma, thank you for passing down your recipes, your wisdom, and your unwavering belief that good food doesn't have to be expensive—it just has to be made with care and love.

To my best friend and loving husband, thank you for enjoying the food I make and for being my biggest supporter in the kitchen. Knowing that you look forward to my cooking makes it all the more rewarding. I love cooking for you—and I love you.

Bringing this cookbook to life was truly a team effort, and I am deeply grateful to the talented individuals who made it possible.

To my editor, Patrik Bass, thank you for your thoughtful guidance, sharp eye, and unwavering support throughout the process. Your insight and patience helped shape this book into something far better than I could have imagined.

To my culinary team Anna Hampton and Jessica Grossman—your attention to detail and dedication ensured each picture was flawless. I am so thankful for your commitment and care.

To my photographer, Sully Sullivan, your ability to capture the heart of each dish is nothing short of magic. The warmth and joy you brought to every image elevated this book to another level! Forever grateful for you!

To my writer, Ylonda Gault, thank you for turning our countless conversations into a cohesive, inviting experience for readers. Your creativity and professionalism were invaluable from start to finish.

And to the entire production and publishing team—thank you for your hard work behind the scenes. Your collaboration and expertise helped transform this vision into reality.

This cookbook is a reflection of many hands, hearts, and shared passions. I'm truly honored to have worked with such a dedicated and inspiring team.

Finally, to everyone looking to feed their loved ones well without breaking the bank—this book is for you. May it help make mealtimes easier, more joyful, and always full of flavor.

universal conversion chart

Oven Temperature Equivalents

250°F = 120°C
400°F = 200°C
275°F = 135°C
425°F = 220°C
300°F = 150°C
450°F = 230°C
325°F = 160°C
475°F = 240°C
350°F = 180°C
500°F = 260°C
375°F = 190°C

Measurement Equivalents

Measurements should always be level unless directed otherwise.

⅛ teaspoon = 0.5 mL

¼ teaspoon = 1 mL

½ teaspoon = 2.5 mL

1 teaspoon = 5 mL

1 tablespoon = 3 teaspoons = ½ fluid ounce = 15 mL

2 tablespoons = ⅛ cup = 1 fluid ounce = 30 mL

4 tablespoons = ¼ cup = 2 fluid ounces = 60 mL

5⅓ tablespoons = ⅓ cup = 3 fluid ounces = 80 mL

8 tablespoons = ½ cup = 4 fluid ounces = 120 mL

10⅔ tablespoons = ⅔ cup = 5 fluid ounces = 160 mL

12 tablespoons = ¾ cup = 6 fluid ounces = 180 mL

16 tablespoons = 1 cup = 8 fluid ounces = 240 mL

Page references in *italics* refer to photos of recipes.

about the author

Kardea Brown is a contemporary Southern chef, author of the *New York Times* bestseller *The Way Home*, and the creator of the New Gullah Supper Club pop-up, where her menu pays homage to dishes her grandmother and mother passed down to her. She is the host of the hit show *Delicious Miss Brown* and *Kids Baking Championship*. She is also a resident judge on *Spring Baking Championship* and cohosted seasonal specials, including *Kids Baking Championship Thanksgiving* in 2023. Kardea lives in Charleston, South Carolina, with her husband, Bryon, and their fur baby, Rhubarb.

HarperCollins books may be purchased for educational, business, or sales promotional use. For information, please email the Special Markets Department at SPsales@harpercollins.com.

harpercollins.com

FIRST EDITION

Designed by Bonni Leon-Berman

All photographs by Sully Sullivan unless otherwise noted.
Page iv by Julieta Amezcua
Page 20 courtesy of the author

Library of Congress Cataloging-in-Publication Data has been applied for.

25 26 27 28 29 LBC 5 4 3 2 1